NIHONGO NO KISO I

—Grammatical Notes—

THE ASSOCIATION FOR OVERSEAS TECHNICAL SCHOLARSHIP

This is the Grammatical Notes in English for NIHONGO NO KISO I

Edited by
Kaigai Gijutsusha Kenshū Kyōkai
(The Association for Overseas Technical Scholarship)
30-1, Senju Azuma 1-chome, Adachi-ku, Tokyo, Japan

Published by
3A Corporation
Shoei Bldg.
6-3, Sarugaku-cho, 2chome, Chiyoda-ku, Tokyo, 101 Japan
Printed in Japan

Preface

This volume contains Grammatical Notes based on the contents of the textbook NIHONGO NO KISO. In NIHONGO NO KISO, sentence pattens for each lesson are arranged from the less difficult to the more difficult so that learners can learn systematically. Also, **Renshū A** in each lesson reintroduces all the new basic sentence patterns that appeared in that lesson. There is, therefore, no special need for publishing a separate volume on grammar; nevertheless, we decided to compile a brief explanatory volume on grammatical points in each lesson, because it does help learners to understand the language much better.

The purpose of this book, then, is to explain sentence patterns in each lesson as simply as possible with minimum use of grammatical terms. The explanation does not go into extremely detailed points or matters of interest only to a grammarian, because this book is written for beginners of the language.

We suggest that learners can use this book most effectively under the guidance of their Japanese language instructors.

Grammatical Notes was compiled by a Japanese language instructor from AOTS, adopting a method of *Practical Japanese Conversation*, a former textbook of AOTS, and it was then revised by Prof. Tomio Kubota, assistant professor of Tokyo University of Foreign Studies.

1st May, 1975

Tokuji Shōji
managing Director
Association for Overseas Technical Scholarship

CONTENTS

Notations used to show word-categories are as follows:

N	*noun* (**meishi**)
	e.g. **tsukue** *desk*
	kenshūsei *trainee*
A	i-*adjective* (**i-keiyōshi**)
	e.g. **atsui** *hot*
	takai *high*
Na	na-*adjective* (**na-keiyōshi**)
	e.g. **shizuka-na** *quiet*
Adv	*adverb* (**fukushi**)
	e.g. **taihen** *very*
	hakkiri *clearly*
V	*verb* (**dōshi**)
	e.g. **kakimasu** *write*
	yomimasu *read*
P	*particle* (**joshi**)
	e.g. **ga, o, no**
Conj	*conjunction* (**setsuzokushi**)
	e.g. **shikashi** *but*
	soshite *and*
m	*modifier*
Obj	*object*

1. General features of Japanese

1. In a sentence, a predicate always comes at the end.
2. A verb has no ending to indicate person and number.
3. There is no article used with nouns in most cases.
4. One and the same form of a noun may mean both the singular and the plural form.
5. The grammatical case of a noun or a pronoun is indicated by means of various particles occurring after the noun or the pronoun.
6. Subject and object are often omitted if they are understood from the context.
7. There are plain and polite styles in Japanese. In daily conversation, either of them may be used depending upon the situation.

2. Japanese Script

We use three kinds of Japanese writing symbols **kanji** (the Chinese ideographic script), **hiragana** and **katakana** (syllabic script).

The Japanese sentence is usually written with a combination of **kanji** and **hiragana**. Foreign names and words of foreign derivation are usually written in **katakana**. Besides the above-mentioned scripts **rōmaji** (Roman letters) is used. This is, however, not usually used, except in dictionaries or on signboards.

1. **rōmaji** ....**Nihongo**   *the Japanese language*
    kanji ....日本語   〃
    hiragana ....にほんご   〃
    katakana ....ニホンゴ   〃
2. *I study Japanese at Kenshū Center.*
    Watashi wa Kenshū Sentā de Nihongo o benkyō-shimasu.
    私は 研修センターで 日本語を 勉強します。
    ○□ ○ △ □ ○ □ ○ □
        ○......**kanji**
        □......**hiragana**
        △......**katakana**

3. Pronunciation of Japanese

Japanese syllables

Japanese syllables are shown in the list in **Nihongo no Kiso** (p. 1).

A typical Japanese syllable consists either of a single vowel or a consonant followed by a vowel. Other special types of syllables will be mentioned later.

A. Vowels (**boin**)

1) Short vowels

a   It is pronounced like **a** in *father*. (But it is shorter)

i   It is pronounced like **i** in *machine*.

u   It is pronounced like **u** in *book*. (**u** is pronounced without lip-rounding)

e   It is pronounced like **e** in *pet*. (But it is shorter)

o   It is pronounced like **o** in *horse*. (But it is shorter)

2) Long vowels

The long and short vowels are in contrast. In the Romanized transcription (**Romaji**), a long vowel is generally marked by a bar above it, except in the case of **i**.

short vowel: **a**   **i**   **u**   **e**   **o**

long vowel: **ā**   **ii**   **ū**   **ē**   **ō**

English-speaking people often neglect the distinction between long and short vowels, but this distinction is very important in Japanese because a change in the length of the vowel changes the meaning of the word.

tokei	*clock*
tōkei	*statistics*

B. Consonants (**shi-in**)

1) Sounds of **n**

There is a special type of nasal sound **n** which constitutes one syllable in Japanese. The sound of **n** varies depending upon the following sound.

/n/	before t, d, n,	**onna, undō, antei**
/m/	before m, p, b,	**bunmei, sanpo, shinbun**
/ŋ/	before k, g, and vowels, etc.	**sankai, kangaemasu**

2) Sounds of **g**

When **g** appears in a initial position, it is pronounced similarly to the hard English /g/. When **g** appears in positions other than a initial position, plosive /g/ changes into nasal /ŋ/, the sound similar to *ng* in *singer*.

But some Japanese don't use nasal /ŋ/, always pronouncing *g* as the hard English /g/, so it is not absolutely necessary to use /ŋ/ because the hard /g/ can be used instead.

3) Double Consonants

Some consonants (k, t, s, p, etc.) also occur as *double consonants*, which are distinguished from their single counterparts by their length. Compare the following. Listen to the tape carefully.

- **oto**   *sound* (o-to: 2 syllables)
- **otto**   *husband* (o-t-to: 3 syllables)
- **shite** (**shi-te**) **imasu**   *be doing*...
- **shitte** (**shi-t-te**) **imasu**   *know*

4) Consonant+**ya, yu, yo** or **sh, ch, ts** + vowel.

   kya, kyu, kyo, sha, ... are of one syllable.

5) **za, zu, zo** and **ja, ju, jo**

   za /za/ **zu** /zu/ **zo** /zo/   **ja** /jza/ **ju** /jzu/ **jo** /jzo/

6) **su** and **tsu**

The sounds are similar, so it may be difficult for foreigners to distinguish them. Please listen to the tape carefully and practice hearing the distinction.

C. Speech rhythm

1) The speech rhythm of Japanese is what we call the *syllable-timed rhythm*, each syllable being pronounced with approximately the same length, except for long vowels, which are approximately twice as long as other syllables.

There is no sharp contrast between stressed and unstressed syllables as in English and some other languages, but a relative pitch level may sometimes signal differences in the meanings of two words.

- **hashi**   *bridge*   **kiru**   *to wear*
- **hashi**   *chopstick*   **kiru**   *to cut*

D. Devocalization of the Vowels

Vowels **i** and **u** are often devoiced (*whispered*) between some voiceless consonants or at the end of a word when the vowel **i** or **u** is preceded by one of these voiceless consonants.

tsu̶kue   *desk*
su̶ki   *like*
ki̶kimasu̶   *listen*
desu̶   *be*

— 3 —

Dai 1 ka

1. Noun [N]

   In Japanese, grammatical number (singular or plural), and gender (masculine or feminine) are not generally marked, although there are some words which express plurality.

2. Particle [P]... **wa, mo, ka,** etc.

   A noun is followed by a particle which expresses a grammatical relation in a sentence.

   1) | N wa |

   This means that a noun is *a topic* or *a subject* of the sentence.

   Watashi wa kenshūsei desu.   *I am a trainee.*

   2) | N mo | N *also*...

   Tanaka-san wa Nihon-jin desu.   *Mr. Tanaka is a Japanese.*

   Kimura-san mo Nihon-jin desu.   *Mr. Kimura is also a Japanese.*

   3) | Sentence | ka...1

   Generally speaking, a sentence can be made into a question by adding **ka** to the end. The interrogative sentence usually has a rising intonation.

   Anata wa kenshūsei desu ka.   *Are you a trainee?*

   4) | N no | (See Lesson 2 and 3.)

3. **desu** (Copula)

   1) The copula is like a be-verb in English, and is used at the end of a sentence. It expresses some kind of polite statement.

   Watashi wa kenshūsei desu.   *I am a trainee.*

   2) The copula is also used in order to make a sentence polite in some cases.

4. Inflection of **desu** in non-past tense.

affirmative	**desu**
negative	***dewa arimasen**

   * In daily conversation, **jā arimasen,** a more colloquial form is usually used.

5. **Hai, sō desu. Iie, sō dewa arimasen.**

sō is often used to answer a question, instead of repeating a <u>noun</u> or a <u>pronoun</u> used in the original question. Thus, the Japanese response may be very simple. Notice that, however, **sō** is not used for replacing a <u>verb</u> or an <u>adjective.</u>

Anata wa Tōkyō Kikai no kenshūsei desu ka.

Are you a trainee of Tōkyō Kikai Co., Ltd.?

Hai, <u>Tōkyō Kikai no kenshūsei</u> desu.
Hai, <u>sō</u> desu. } *Yes, I am.*

Iie, <u>Tōkyō Kikai no kenshūsei</u> dewa arimasen.
Iie, <u>sō</u> dewa arimasen. } *No, I am not.*

6. **-san**

In Japanese, **-san** is attached after personal names when addressing of referring to other people. It is never attached by the speaker to his own name.

Watashi wa Kimura desu.   *I am Kimura.*

Anata wa Tanaka-<u>san</u> desu ka.   *Are you* { *Mr.* / *Mrs.* / *Miss* } *Tanaka?*

Tanaka Haruo	full name
Tanaka	family name
Haruo	given name

In Japanese, the full name or the family name is usually used in speaking to or about another person. The given name alone is usually used only among very close friends or within a family.

7. Position of Interrogative word

In Japanese, an interrogative word is used in the same position that a non-interrogative noun would be used in the declarative sentence.

Anata wa | Rao-san | **desu ka.**   *Are you* | Mr. Rao | *?*
Anata wa | dare | **desu ka.** | Who | *are you?*

8. **dare** and **donata**

Both **dare** and **donata** mean *who*, but **donata** is more polite than **dare.**

9. **ohayō gozaimasu**

This means *good morning.* **ohayō** is the short form, and is used when we speak to a friend or an inferior, not to a superior.

Dai 2 ka

1. <u>Demonstrative words</u>

   1) **kore, sore, are**

      kore indicates a thing belonging to, or nearer to a speaker than to a listener.

      sore indicates a thing belonging to, or nearer to the listener than to a speaker.

      are indicates a thing belonging neither to a speaker nor to a listener or something separated from both a speaker and a listener.

   2) **kono, sono, ano**

      kore, sore and **are** become **kono, sono** and **ano** when immediately followed by a noun.

      kono hon   *this book*

2. | N no N |...1   *my book, etc., somebody's book, etc., a book, etc. of ...*

   The particle **no** connects a noun with another noun, like *of* in English (though order of two nouns is the reverse of that in English.)

      watashi no hon   *my book* (possessive)

      Sentā no basu   *Center's bus* (possessive)

3. | N no | *mine, somebody's, a thing of ...*

   This construction expresses the possessor. The noun following **no** (as in the examples of sec. 2 above) is often omitted when it is understood from the context.

Kore wa anata no hon desu ka.	*Is this your book?*
Hai, watashi no (hon) desu.	*Yes, it is mine.*
Are wa dare no jidōsha desu ka.	*Whose car is that?*
Sentā no (jidōsha) desu.	*It belongs to the Center.*
	or *It is the Center's.*

4. **-sai**

   When referring to person's age, an auxiliary numeral **-sai** is attached after the number indicating the age.

   The interrogative word is **nan-sai** or **(o)ikutsu.**

   Anata wa $\left\{ \begin{array}{l} \text{nan-sai} \\ \text{*(o)ikutsu} \end{array} \right\}$ **desu ka.**   *How old are you?*

— 6 —

(See Lesson 11 and appendix 1.)
    * (o)ikutsu ... o is an honorific prefix.

Watashi wa 34-sai desu.   *I am 34 years old.*

5. **-ban**

   -ban is an auxiliary numerals showing order.   (See Lesson 11 and appendix 1.)

     Nan-ban desu ka.   *What number?*

     5-ban desu.   *Five.*

Dai 3 ka

1. **koko, soko, asoko, doko**
   kochira, sochira, achira, dochira

   The pronouns **kore, sore** and **are** are used to refer to a thing; **koko, soko, asoko** and **doko** are used to refer to a place. **kochira, sochira, achira** and **dochira** are used to refer to a direction or a place. **kochira, sochira** and **achira** are more polite expressions than **koko, soko** and **asoko**. **kochira, sochira** and **achira** are also used as a polite expression in place of **kono hito, sono hito** and **ano hito**. (See NIHONGO NO KISO Lesson 19. Kaiwa)

2. $\boxed{\text{N no N}}$ ...2

   The particle **no** connects N with another N, as mentioned in Lesson 2, but there are other meanings or uses of **no** in addition to that explained in lesson 2. Compare the following Japanese and English phrases.

   1) **Nihon no jidōsha**   *a car made in Japan.*
   2) **Nihon-go no hon**   *a book (which is written) in Japanese* or
                                   a book on the Japanese language.
   3) **onna no hito**   *a person (who is) female. (=a woman)*
   4) **Tai no Tanom**   *Tanom from Thailand.*
   5) **Tomodachi no Lee-san**   *My friend, Mr. Lee.*

3. **doko, dochira**

   Anata no kaisha wa $\left\{\begin{array}{c}\text{doko}\\\text{dochira}\end{array}\right\}$ **desu ka.**

   This sentence has two meanings. One is asking a location of the company (1, below), and the other is asking a name of the company (2, below). Usually, this sentence is used when a name of the company is the information being asked about by a speaker.

   Anata no kaisha wa $\left\{\begin{array}{c}\text{doko}\\\text{dochira}\end{array}\right\}$ **desu ka.**

   (1) *Where is your company?*
   (2) *What is the name of your company?*

   In asking the name of a person's company, **Anata no kaisha wa nan desu ka.** is *not* used.

4. Demonstrative pronouns, adjectives

demonstrative pronoun	demonstrative adjective	pronoun of place	pronoun indicating direction, side, place
kore (*this*)	**kono** (*this*)	**koko** (*this place*)	**kochira** (*this direction, side, place*)
sore (*that*)	**sono** (*that*) $\Big\}$ +N	**soko** (*that place*)	**sochira** (*that direction, side, place*)
are (*that over there*)	**ano** (*that over there*)	**asoko** (*that place over there*)	**achira** (*that direction, side, place over there*)
dore (*which*)	**dono** (*which*)+N	**doko** (*where*)	**dochira** $\left(\begin{array}{l}where \\ which\ direction\end{array}\right)$

5. Particle **to** ... 1.

This means *and*.

> **sensei to kenshūsei**　　　　　*a teacher and a trainee*

Both **to** and **soshite** mean *and*. However, **to** is used to connect two nouns, whereas **soshite** two sentences.

> **hon to enpitsu**　　　　　*a book and a pencil*
> **Kore wa hon desu, soshite**　　*This is a book, and*
> **sore wa enpitsu desu.**　　　　*that is a pencil.*

6. **ikura**

ikura is an interrogative word asking a price. (or quantity.)

> **Kore wa ikura desu ka.**　　*How much is this?*

7. ⃞Sentence⃞ **ka** ... 2

When a final particle **ka** is added to the end of a sentence, it sometimes means something like *Oh, I see*. In this case, the particle has a falling intonation.

> **Sō desu ka.**　　　　　*Oh, I see.*
> **Kenshūsei desu ka.**　　*(He is) a trainee, I see.*

8. ⃞Sentence⃞ **ne**

The final particle **ne** asks for a listener's approval and is similar in function to such English structures as *isn't it?, aren't you?, doesn't he?, right?* etc.

> **Lee-san to onaji desu ne.**　*It's the same as Mr. Lee, isn't it?*

Dai 4 ka

1. -masu

In all sentences, final verbs end with **-masu** in ordinary polite speech.

okimasu	*get up*
nemasu	*sleep*
hatarakimasu	*work*

-masu is inflected for tense and mood.

2. Inflection of -masu

	non-past (present, future)	past
affirmative	(oki)-**masu**	(oki)-**mashita**
negative	(oki)-**masen**	(oki)-**masendeshita**
volitional	*(oki)-**mashō**	

The non-past form is used to refer to both present and future actions and states. Japanese does not distinguish between the two grammatically.

Watashi wa mainichi hatarakimasu.	*I work everyday.*
Watashi wa ashita hatarakimasu.	*I will work tomorrow.*

* (oki)-**mashō** (See Lesson 6)

3. Particle ni...1

N(time) **ni**	*at* (time)

After a noun which expresses time, the particle **ni** is used.

Watashi wa 6-ji ni okimasu.	*I get up at 6 o'clock.*
Watashi wa nichi-yōbi ni benkyō-shimasen.	*I don't study on Sunday.*

ni is omitted after the following words **itsu** *when*, **kinō** *yesterday*, **kyō** *today*, **ashita** *tomorrow*, **senshū** *last week*, **konshū** *this week*, **raishū** *next week*, **kyonen** *last year*, **kotoshi** *this year*, **rainen** *next year*.

kinō ~~ni~~ hatarakimashita.	*Yesterday, I worked.*

4. **-ji, -fun (-pun)**

These are the auxiliary numerals for time. (See appendix 1)

-ji	*o'clock*	ichi-ji	*one o'clock*
		ni-ji	*two* 〃
		san-ji	*three* 〃
		yo-ji	*four* 〃 (Don't say **shi-ji** or **yon-ji**)
		go-ji	*five* 〃
		roku-ji	*six* 〃
		nana-ji } shichi-ji }	*seven* 〃
		hachi-ji	*eight* 〃
		ku-ji	*nine* 〃 (Don't say **kyū-ji**)
		jū-ji	*ten* 〃
		jūichi-ji	*eleven* 〃
		jūni-ji	*twelve* 〃
		nan-ji	*what time?*

-fun *minute(s)* **-fun** changes into **-pun** depending upon the numeral that preceeds **-fun.**

	ip-pun	*one minute*	
	ni-fun	*two minutes*	
	san-pun	*three* 〃	
	yon-pun	*four* 〃	(Don't say **shi-fun**
	go-fun	*five* 〃	or **yo-fun**)
	rop-pun	*six* 〃	
	nana-fun	*seven* 〃	
	hap-pun	*eight* 〃	
	kyū-fun	*nine* 〃	(Don't say **ku-fun**)
	jup-pun	*ten* 〃	
	nan-pun	*how many minutes?*	

5. benkyō; benkyō-shimasu

   benkyō *study* is a noun, benkyō-shimasu *to study* is a verb.   Many nouns
   which refer to actions become verbs by adding -shimasu *do*.
   N-shimasu belongs to the third group verbs.   (See Lesson 14)

   Watashi wa <u>Nihon-go no benkyō</u> o <u>shimasu</u>=
   N (object)   V

   Watashi wa <u>Nihon-go</u> o <u>benkyō-shimasu</u>.
   N (object)   V

   I study Japanese   or   *I am going to study Japanese.*

   Ashita no <u>benkyō</u> wa nan-ji kara desu ka.=
   N

   Ashita nan-ji kara <u>benkyo-shimasu</u> ka.
   V

   What time will you have class tomorrow?

6. Particle ... kara ... made

   | N (time or place) **kara** N (time or place) **made** | *from ... ta ...*

   1) (time) **kara** (time) **made** means   *from a certain time to a certain time.*
      9-ji <u>kara</u> 12-ji <u>made</u> benkyō-shimasu.
      I study from 9 to 12.
      Asa <u>kara</u> ban <u>made</u> hatarakimasu.
      I work from morning till evening.

   2) (place) **kara** (place) **made** means   *from one place to another place.*
      (See NIHONGO NO KISO, Lesson 5, **Reibun** 6, p. 29)
      Ōsaka <u>kara</u> Nagoya <u>made</u> jidōsha de ikimasu.
      I will go by car from Osaka to Nagoya.

Dai 5 ka

1. Particle **e**

| N (place) **e** | $I \begin{Bmatrix} come \\ go \\ return \end{Bmatrix}$ to (place) |

The particle **e** marks the noun indicating direction, and is used with verbs which have a directional meaning such as **ikimasu, kimasu, kaerimasu.**

    Watashi wa Kyōto e ikimasu.   *I will go to Kyoto.*

The particle **ni**, which makes the noun showing the point of arrival, is sometimes used instead of **e.**

    Watashi wa Kyōto ni ikimasu.   *I will go to Kyoto.*

2. $\left. \begin{matrix} \textbf{doko (e)} \\ \textbf{(ni)} \\ \textbf{dare} \\ \textbf{nani} \end{matrix} \right\}$ **mo ...-masen** (negative)   *I don't ...* $\begin{Bmatrix} anywhere \\ anybody \\ anything \end{Bmatrix}$

| Interrogative pronoun (particle) **mo** negative |

When interrogative pronouns are immediately followed by **mo** which is in turn followed by a negative, they lose their interrogative meaning, and they signal a complete negative.

    Doko (e) mo ikimasen.   *(I) don't go anywhere.*

    Dare mo kimasen.   *Nobody comes.*

    Nani mo tabemasen.   *(I) eat nothing.* (See Lesson 6.)

3. Particle **de ... 1**

| N (vehicle) **de** | *by (bus, train, etc.)* |

The particle **de** following N expresses means of transportation.

    Densha de ikimasu.   *(I) will go by train.*

4. Particle **to ... 2**

| N (person) **to** [**issho ni**] | *with (a friend, etc.)* |

The particle **to** following a noun means *with* N, or *accompanied by* N. **issho ni** can be omitted.

    Tomodachi to [issho ni] ikimasu.

        (I) will go with my friend.

5. **V-masen ka**

There are different uses for this pattern.

1) **ikimasen ka.**   Do you not...?

The first use, as shown in the above example, is to ask whether the listener will go or not.

The answer to this question is,

    Hai, ikimasen.   *No, I will not go.*

    Iie, ikimasu.   *Yes, I will go.*

The usage of **hai,** and **iie** is different from that of English. (See Lesson 7.)

2) **ikimasen ka.**   Won't you...?

The second use for this type of question is not to ask whether the listener will go or not, but to invite the listener to go. (with the speaker)

    Ikimasen ka.   *Won't you go?* (with me or with us)

    Hai, ikimashō.   *Yes, let's go.*

Dai 6 ka

1. Particle **o** . . . 1

   | N **o** V (transitive) |

   The particle **o** appearing before a transitive verb (**tabemasu** *eat*, **tsukurimasu** *make*, etc.), shows the object of the verb.

       Nihon-go o benkyō-shimasu.   *study Japanese*

       gohan o tabemasu.   *eat a meal*

2. Particle **de** . . . 2

   | N (place) **de** [N **o**] V (action) | *I do [something] at (place)*

   The particle **de** following a place noun marks the noun as the place where an action occurs.

       Kenshū Sentā de Nihon-go o benkyō-shimasu.

       (I) study Japanese at the Kenshu Center.

3. **nan** and **nani**

   Both of them mean *what* **nan** is used in the following cases and **nani** in other cases.

      1) when the following word is initiated with d, n or t.

        nan desu ka   *What is (it)?*   (Lesson 2)

        nan no hon   *What book?*   (Lesson 3)

        nan to iimashita ka *What did (he) say?*   (See Lesson 21)

      2) when it is used with an auxiliary numeral.

        nan-sai   *how old?*   (Lesson 2)

        nan-ban   *what number?*   (Lesson 2)

4. **V-mashō** . . . 1

   This is the volitional form of the verb.   Meaning is *let's* . . .

       Ikimashō.   *Let's go.*

5. **donokurai** (or **donogurai**)

   This form sometimes means *how long?* However, depending upon the situation and the predicate following it, **donokurai** may mean *how long?*, *how far?*, *how much?*, *how many?*. **donokurai** is used in various cases, such as asking a price, a quantity, a number, etc. (See NIHONGO NO KISO,

— 15 —

Lesson 11, **Kaiwa**, p. 64) **nan**+auxiliary numeral (+**gurai**) is also used instead of **donokurai**.

Koko kara Ginza made <u>**donokurai**</u> **kakarimasu ka.**

How long does it take from here to Ginza?

Koko kara Ginza made nan-pun (+**gurai**) **kakarimasu ka.**

(About) how many minutes does it take from here to Ginza?

Dai 7 ka

1. Particle **de** ... 3

$$\boxed{\text{N}\begin{pmatrix}\text{tool}\\\text{method}\end{pmatrix}\;\textbf{de}}\qquad with\ldots,\ in\ldots,\ by\ldots$$

The particle **de** following a noun marks the noun as the instrument, tool, means, or method which is used in performing an action.

      Hashi <u>de</u> gohan o tabemasu.   *(I) eat with chopsticks.*

      Nihon-go <u>de</u> kakimasu.   *(I) write in Japanese.*

2. Particle **ni** ... 2

$$\boxed{\text{N}_1\begin{pmatrix}\text{person}\\\text{place}\end{pmatrix}\;\textbf{ni}\;\text{N}_2\;\textbf{o}\;\textbf{agemasu, etc.}}\qquad (I)\ will\ give\ \text{N}_2\ to\ \text{N}_1$$

Some verbs, such as **agemasu** *give*, **okurimasu** *send*, **denwa o kakemasu** *make a telephone call*, etc. may occur with a direct object and an indirect object. The direct object is marked by the particle **o** following the noun.

The indirect object is marked by the particle **ni** following the noun.

      Watashi wa <u>Tanom-san ni</u> <u>hon o</u> agemasu.
                (indirect obj) (direct obj)

      I will give a book to Mr. Tanom.

3. Particle **ni** ... 3

$$\boxed{\text{N}_1\begin{pmatrix}\text{person}\\\text{place}\end{pmatrix}\begin{Bmatrix}\textbf{kara}\\\textbf{ni}\end{Bmatrix}\text{N}_2\;\textbf{o}\;\textbf{moraimasu, etc.}}\qquad (I)\ receive\ \text{N}_2\ from\ \text{N}_1$$

With some verbs, such as **moraimasu** *receive*, **naraimasu** *learn*, etc., **kara** or **ni** occurs after the person or place which influences or gives something to the subject of the sentence; that is, the particles **kara** or **ni** mark the source of the thing received by the subject of the sentence.

      Watashi wa tomodachi $\begin{Bmatrix}\textbf{kara}\\\textbf{ni}\end{Bmatrix}$ **tokei o moraimashita.**

      I received a watch from my friend.

    N (person) $\begin{Bmatrix}\textbf{kara}\\\textbf{ni}\end{Bmatrix}$ **moraimashita.** *(I) received (something) from a person.*

    N (place, company) **kara moraimashita.** *(I) received (something) from a*
                                     company.

      <u>Dare</u> $\begin{Bmatrix}\textbf{kara}\\\textbf{ni}\end{Bmatrix}$ **moraimashita ka.**   *From whom did you receive (it)?*

      <u>Tanaka-san</u> $\begin{Bmatrix}\textbf{kara}\\\textbf{ni}\end{Bmatrix}$ **moraimashita.**   *I received (it) from Mr. Tanaka*

<u>Doko kara</u> moraimashita ka.	*From which company or place did you receive (it)?*
Watashi no <u>kaisha kara</u> morai-mashita.	*I received (it) from my company.*

4. <u>mō</u> and <u>mada</u>

mō V-mashita	*(I) did (it) or (I) have already done (it).*
mada V-masen	*(I) have not done it yet.*

1) **V-mashita, V-masendeshita** indicate that an action or state was done or was not done at a certain point or period in the past.

Kinō tegami o kakimashita ka.	*Did you write the letter yesterday?*
Hai, kakimashita.	*Yes, I did.*
Iie, kakimasendeshita.	*No, I didn't.*

2) **V-mashita** also shows that an action or state has just now been completed. In such a case, the corresponding negative form **V-masendeshita** is not used, because the action or state did not come about in the past and still has not come about, so the negative concept is a matter of the present. Therefore, present tense is used.

Tegami o kakimashita ka.	*Have you written the letter?*
Hai, <u>mō</u> kakimashita.	*Yes, I have already written it.*
Iie, <u>mada</u> kakimasen.	*No, I have not written it yet.*
cf. Mō tabemashita.	*I already ate.*
Mō tabemasu.	*(I am) going to eat now.*
Mō tabemashō.	*Let's eat now.*
Mō tabemasen.	*I can't eat any more (because, I have already eaten enough.)*

5. <u>hai, ē,</u> and <u>iie</u>

hai, ē and **iie** are all used in response to questions. **hai** and **ē** mean something like *what you have said or implied is correct*, and **iie** means something like *what you have said or implied is not correct*. In Japanese, a negative question, for example **ikimasen ka**, *Aren't you going?* is used when the speaker expects that the listener will answer that he is not going. Similarly an affirmative question, for example **ikimasu ka**, *Are you going?* is used when the speaker expects that the listener will answer that he is going. Therefore when the listener is in fact going to do that which agrees with the questioner's expectation the listener answers **hai** or **ē**, and when he is going to do that which does not agree with the questioner's expectation, he answers

iie. hai and **ē** are translated sometimes by *yes* and sometimes by *no*; **iie** is also translated sometimes by *yes* and sometimes by *no*, depending on what kind of question was asked.   Note the following examples:

Ginza e ikimasu ka.	*Will you go to Ginza?*
—**Hai,** —**Ē,** } **ikimasu.**	*Yes, I will.*
—**Iie, ikimasen.**	*No, I will not.*
Ginza e ikimasen ka.	*Will you not go to Ginza?*
—**Hai,** —**Ē,** } **ikimasen.**	*No, I will not.*
—**Iie, ikimasu.**	*Yes, I will.*

Both **hai** and **ē** may be used in answer to questions as shown in the above examples, but **ē** is not as stiff and formal as **hai** and so **ē** occurs more often in daily conversation.   However, **hai** is used to answer when one's name is called or when there is a knock on the door. **ē** is not used in such cases.

Rao-san!	*Mr. Rao!*
—**Hai.**	*Yes.*

6. | N (place) **ni tsukimasu** | (*I*) *arrive in...*

Particle **ni** is used to mark the place.

Kinō Tōkyō <u>ni</u> tsukimashita.   *Yesterday, (he) arrived in Tokyo.*

Dai 8 ka

Adjectives

1. In Japanese, there are two kinds of adjectives:
    1) i-adjective [A]
    2) na-adjective [Na]

2. i-adjectives are so called because they all end with -i (following a, i, u, o.) in a plain style (dictionary form) of the word.

atsui	*hot*	**omoi**	*heavy*
ōkii	*big*	**chiisai**	*small*

    i-adjectives can be used as the predicate of a sentence, or can modify a noun when they occur before the noun in a sentence.

    Kore wa oishii ringo desu. *This is a delicious apple.*

    (modifier)

    Kono ringo wa oishii desu. *This apple is delicious.*
    (predicate)

3. na-adjectives are also used as the predicate or the modifier.

shinsetsu	*kind*	**kirei**	*beautiful*
shizuka	*quiet*	**yūmei**	*famous*

    na-adjectives look like ordinary nouns when used as the predicate of a sentence, but they take the form of ...-na when used as modifiers of a following noun.

    Sakura wa kireina hana desu. *Cherry blossoms are beautiful flowers.*

    (modifier)

    Sakura wa kirei desu. *Cherry blossoms are beautiful.*
    (predicate)

4. Negative of Adjectives

  1) The negative form of i-adjectives is

    stem-ku -nai desu

      oishii   (plain affirmative form (See Lesson 20))
        ↓
      oishi-   (*stem)
        ↓
      oishi-ku-nai   (plain negative form (See Lesson 20))
        ↓
      oishikunai desu   (polite negative form)
        or
      oishiku(wa) arimasen (″   )

        * The stem is the main part of a word to which various endings may
          be added. The stem of an i-adjective is formed by deleting final i.

  2) The negative form of **na**-adjective is the same as the negative form of a
     noun.

    stem + dewa arimasen

      kirei   (stem)
        ↓
      kirei desu   (polite affirmative)
        ↓
      kirei dewa arimasen (polite negative)

5. Inflection of adjectives

	non-past	
	i-adjective	na-adjective
affirmative	**takai desu**	**shizuka desu**
negative	**takakunai desu**	**shizuka dewa arimasen**

affirmative	negative
Kono hon wa takai desu.	⟶**Kono hon wa takakunai desu.**
This book is expensive.	*This book is not expensive.*
Kore wa takai hon desu.	⟶**Kore wa takai hon dewa arimasen.**
This is an expensive book.	*This is not an expensive book.*
Kono machi wa shizuka desu.	⟶**Kono machi wa shizuka dewa arimasen.**
This town is quiet.	*This town is not quiet.*
Koko wa shizukana machi desu.	⟶**Koko wa shizukana machi dewa arimasen.**
This is a quiet town.	*This is not a quiet town.*

6. **amari... masen** (*negative*)

> amari A-ku nai desu
>
> amari Na dewa arimasen } *not so...*

amari, when used with a negative, has the meaning *not so...* or *not very....*

> Kyō wa <u>amari</u> atsu<u>kunai</u> desu.   *It is not so hot today.*
>
> Koko wa <u>amari</u> shizuka <u>dewa arimasen</u>.   *This place is not so quiet.*

7. <u>donna</u>

donna is an interrogative word asking a state.

> <u>Donna</u> hon desu ka.   *What kind of book is it?*
>
> <u>Omoshiroi</u> hon desu.   *It is an interesting book.*
>   A
>
> c.f. <u>Nan</u> no hon desu ka.   *What book is it?*
>
>   <u>Jidōsha</u> no hon desu.   *It is a book on automobiles.*
>   N

8. <u>negative of **ii desu**</u>

The negative of **ii desu** is **yokunai desu.**

Notice that **ikunai desu** is not used.

> **Kono kamera wa <u>ii</u> desu.** (affirmative)   *This camera is good.*
>
> **Kono kamera wa <u>yokunai</u> desu.** (negative)   *This camera is not good.*

9. *hot water*

atsui means *hot* and **mizu** means *water,* but we don't say **atsui mizu,** but say (**o**)-**yu** to denote *hot water.*

Dai 9 ka

1.

N₁ wa N₂ ga	suki desu kirai desu jōzu desu heta desu dekimasu wakarimasu irimasu arimasu hoshii desu	N₁	*like* *dislike* *be good at* *be poor at* *can do* (See Lesson 18) *understand* *need* (See Lesson 16) *have* *want* (See Lesson 13)	N₂

Though the Japanese sentence patterns above have been translated into the English sentences shown on the right, it is important to keep in mind that **suki, kirai,** etc. are not exact equivalents to English transitive verbs like *like, dislike* and so forth. The construction N₂ **ga** occurring in Japanese sentences is translated into a direct object in the English equivalent sentence, but N₂ **ga** is not actually an object but is a subject in the Japanese sentence since it differs in behavior from the objects of other sentences which are marked with the particle **o.** N₁ is a topic of a sentence marked by **wa** and N₂ is a subject marked by **ga.** See the following Japanese sentence and its equivalent English.

Tanaka-san wa Ei-go ga jōzu desu.

> *As for Mr. Tanaka, [his] English is good=*
>
> *Mr. Tanaka's English is good=*
>
> *Mr. Tanaka speaks English well.*

>> **suki, kirai, jōzu, heta**.....................**na**-adjective
>> **hoshii** ....**i**-adjective
>> **dekimasu, wakarimasu, irimasu, arimasu**......verb

2.

Sentence Phrase	(stating reason)	kara	*Because..., As..., or ..., so*

Onaka ga itai desu kara, nani mo tabemasen.

> *As I have a stomachache, I'll eat nothing.*

Notice that **kara** comes at the end of the phrase or the sentence which states the reason.

3. **dōshite**

This is an interrogative adverb, and means *Why...?*

Watashi wa ikimasen.	*I will not go.*
Dōshite ikimasen ka.	
Dōshite desu ka.	*Why won't you go?*
Dōshite.	
Atama ga itai desu kara.	*Because I have a headache.*

4. **zenzen...masen** (negative)　　*not...at all*

zenzen is used with negative verb or adjective.

Watashi wa Nihon-go ga zenzen wakarimasen.
   I don't understand Japanese at all.

5. **N, etc. dake**

dake means *only*. Notice that **dake** is used after N, etc.

kenshūsei dake	*only trainees*
100-en dake	*only ¥100*

Dai 10 ka

1. <u>arimasu, imasu</u>

   These verbs are used to express existence. The particle **ga** is usually used with these verbs in patterns shown below.

Hon ga arimasu.	*There is a book.*
Kenshūsei ga imasu.	*There is a trainee.*

   When the subject, which is marked by **ga**, is inanimate, such as **tsukue** *desk*, **tabako** *tobacco,* **hana** *flower*, etc., **arimasu** is used.   When the subject is animate, such as **anata** *you*, **kenshūsei** *trainee*, **inu** *dog*, etc., **imasu** is used.

Tsukue ga arimasu.	*There is a desk.*
Kenshūsei ga imasu.	*There is a trainee.*

2.

N_1 no	koko soko asoko ue shita naka soto mae ushiro migi hidari tonari chikaku aida	ni N_2 ga	arimasu imasu	*There is N_2*	*here* *there* *over there* *on, above* *under, beneath* *in, inside* *out, outside* *in front of* *behind, back* *right* *left* *next (door)* *near* *between, among*	N_1

3. In the above construction, N_2, which is followed by **ga,** is assumed to be something indefinite. When talking about a definite thing (or person), and asking or telling a location or a position of the thing (or person), the following pattern is used instead.

Hon wa doko ni arimasu ka.	*Where is the book?*
Hon wa tsukue no ue ni arimasu.	*The book is on the desk.*

   In this sentence pattern, note that the particle **ga** has been replaced by **wa.**

4.

$$\left.\begin{array}{l}\text{... ni arimasu} \\ \text{... ni imasu}\end{array}\right\} \longrightarrow \text{... desu}$$

    Terebi wa shokudō ni arimasu.   *The television is in the dining hall.*

    Tanaka-san wa jimusho ni imasu.   *Mr. Tanaka is in the office.*

In the above sentence pattern, **... ni arimasu, ... ni imasu** can be replaced by **desu.** (Lesson 3.)

    Terebi wa shokudō desu.   *The television is in the dining hall.*

    Tanaka-san wa jimusho desu.   *Mr. Tanaka is in the office.*

5. $\boxed{\text{N}_1 \text{ to N}_2}$, $\boxed{\text{N}_1 \text{ ya N}_2 \text{ (nado)}}$

Both N_1 **to** N_2 **to** N_3... and N_1 **ya** N_2 **ya** N_3... mean N_1 *and* N_2 *and* N_3... but in the former, it is assumed that one is enumerating the items in the list exhaustively, while in the latter, one is not enumerating all but only some of them. **... nado** means ... *and so on*, or *etc.*

    Tsukue no ue ni hon to pen to haizara ga arimasu.

       There are a book, a pen and an ashtray on the desk.

    Tsukue no ue ni hon ya pen nado ga arimasu.

       There are a book and a pen, etc. on the desk.

Dai 11 ka

Numerals

1. Cardinal numbers

There are two kinds of numerals in Japanese, cardinal numbers and ordinal numbers. The first set is what may be called *Primary Numerals*. These were borrowed from Chinese. The *Primary Numerals* are used in isolation when counting in the abstract, as in mathematics.

    1: **ichi**   2: **ni**   3: **san,...**

The other set of numerals may be called *Secondary Numerals*. They are of native Japanese origin.

    1: **hitotsu**   2: **futatsu**   3: **mittsu,...**

2. Ordinal numbers

There are several ways to express ordinal numbers.

No. 1	dai ichi	No. 2	dai ni
	ichi ban [me]		ni ban [me]
	dai ichi ban [me]		dai ni ban [me]
	hitotsu [me]		futatsu [me]

3. Auxiliary Numerals (**Josūshi**)

When counting things or expressing how many things there are, an *Auxiliary Numeral* is attached to the numeral. The choice of *Auxiliary Numerals* depends upon the thing counted. (See appendix I)

    -mai   for thin, flat objects, such as sheets of paper, dishes, etc.

        1: **ichi-mai**   2: **ni-mai,..**

    -dai   for machines and vehicles, such as cars, typewriters, etc.

        1: **ichi-dai**   2: **ni-dai,..**

    -nin   for persons

        3: **san-nin**   4: **yo-nin,..**

    -fun, -pun   for minute(s)

        1: **ip-pun**   2: **ni-fun,..**

    -jikan   for hour(s)

        1: **ichi-jikan**   2: **ni-jikan,..**

    -nichi   for day(s)

        1: **ichi-nichi**   15: **jūgo-nichi,..**

-shūkan	for week(s)
	1: **is-shūkan** 2: **ni-shūkan**,...
-kagetsu	for month(s)
	1: **ik-kagetsu** 2: **ni-kagetsu**,...
-nen	for year(s)
	1: **ichi-nen** 2: **ni-nen**,...
-sai	for year(s) of age (Lesson 2)
	1: **is-sai** 2: **ni-sai**,...
-kai, -do	number of times (frequency)
	1: **ik-kai, ichi-do** 2: **ni-kai, ni-do**,...
-ban	order in a series (Lesson 2)
	1: **ichi-ban** 2: **ni-ban**,...
-kai, -gai	for floor (Lesson 10)
	1: **ik-kai** 2: **ni-kai** 3: **san-gai**...
-en	for Japanese money (Lesson 3)
	1: **ichi-en** 2: **ni-en**,...
-ka, } **dai...ka** }	for lesson
	1: **ik-ka** or **dai ik-ka** 2: **ni-ka** or **dai ni-ka**,...

4. **nan-** (Auxiliary Numeral)

In asking the number of something, the appropriate Auxiliary Numeral from the above list is used with the form **nan-** in place of a numeral.

    Jidōsha ga <u>nan</u>-dai arimasu ka.   *How many cars are there?*

5. Numeral without an auxiliary numeral

The *Secondary Numerals* are used without any *Auxiliary Numerals*, but only when counting certain kinds of things. For other things the *Primary Numerals + Auxiliary Numerals* are used. *The Secondary Numeral system* (without *Auxiliary Numerals*) goes up only as far as ten.

    Ringo ga <u>futatsu</u> arimasu.   *There are two apples.*

    cf. **Jidōsha ga <u>ni-dai</u> arimasu.**   *There are two cars.*

6. **ikutsu, ikura**

The interrogative form of the secondary numerals is **ikutsu.**

    Hako ga <u>ikutsu</u> arimasu ka.   *How many boxes are there?*

    Mittsu arimasu.   *There are three.*

Notice that **ikutsu** is used when asking the numbers of things, not that of persons; Therefore the following question is not asking the number of persons, but rather the age of a person.

    Anata wa (o)ikutsu desu ka.   *How old are you?* (Lesson 2)

ikura means *How much...?*, and is used to ask a price or an amount. (Lesson 3)

    Kono kamera wa ikura desu ka.   *How much is this camera?*

    Go-man-en desu.   *It is 50,000 yen.*

7. **-ri, -ka**

There are some auxiliary numerals which are used only with the *Secondary Numerals*.

    -ri   for people

        1 : **hitori**   2 : **futari**

    When expressing the number of more than three people, (Primary Numeral)-**nin** should be used:

        3 : **san-nin**   4 : **yo-nin...**

    -ka   for days, dates

        2 : **futsu-ka**   3 : **mik-ka**   4 : **yok-ka**   5 : **itsu-ka**

        6 : **mui-ka**   7 : **nano-ka**   8 : **yō-ka**   9 : **kokono-ka**

        10 : **tō-ka**   14 : **jūyok-ka**   20 : **hatsu-ka**

        24 : **nijūyok-ka** etc.

    For other dates or numbers of days, (Primary Numerals)-**nichi** is used.

8.

Amount (of duration) **ni** Amount (of $\left\{ \begin{array}{l} \text{frequency} \\ \text{duration} \end{array} \right\}$)

    1-nichi ni 3-kai   *three times a day*

    1-shūkan ni 1-do   *once a week*

    1-nichi ni 8-jikan   *eight hours a day*

9. **N -sei**

This means *be made in* N (place) or *be made of* N (material).

    gaikoku-sei   *made in a foreign country*

    nairon-sei   *made of nylon*

Dai 12 ka

Comparison

1. Japanese adjectives are not inflected for *comparative* or *superlative* as are English adjectives. Japanese comparison is expressed by means of particles or adverbs.

2. Comparison between two items

$$\boxed{N_1 \text{ wa } N_2 \text{ yori } \left\{ \begin{array}{c} A \\ Na \end{array} \right\} \text{ desu}} \qquad N_1 \text{ is more } \left\{ \begin{array}{c} A \\ Na \end{array} \right\} \text{ than } N_2.$$

Tōkyō wa Ōsaka yori ōkii desu. *Tokyo is larger than Osaka.*

3. Questions and answers about comparison between two items

   1) Question

   $$\boxed{N_1 \text{ to } N_2 \text{ to dochira ga } \left\{ \begin{array}{c} A \\ Na \end{array} \right\} \text{ desu ka.}} \qquad Which \ is \ more \left\{ \begin{array}{c} A \\ Na \end{array} \right\} N_1 \ or \ N_2?$$

   Tōkyō to Ōsaka to dochira ga ōkii desu ka.
   Which is larger, Tokyo or Osaka?

   Tanom-san to Rao-san to dochira ga wakai desu ka.
   Who is younger Mr. Tanom or Mr. Rao?

   dochira or **dochira no hō ga** can be used in comparing any two items—persons, things, places, time, etc.

   2) Answer

   $$\boxed{N_1 \text{ no hō ga } \left\{ \begin{array}{c} A \\ Na \end{array} \right\} \text{ desu}} \qquad N_1 \text{ is more} \left\{ \begin{array}{c} A \\ Na \end{array} \right.$$

   Tōkyō no hō ga ōkii desu. *Tokyo is larger.*

   Tanom-san no hō ga wakai desu. *Mr. Tanom is younger.*

4. Comparison among more than three items

   $$\boxed{N_1 \text{ to } N_2 \text{ to } N_3 \text{ [no naka] de, } N_1 \text{ ga ichiban} \left\{ \begin{array}{c} A \\ Na \end{array} \right\} \text{ desu}}$$

   $$N_1 \text{ is the most } \left\{ \begin{array}{c} A \\ Na \end{array} \right\} among \ N_1, \ N_2 \ and \ N_3.$$

   Tōkyō to Ōsaka to Kyōto [no naka] de, Tōkyō ga ichiban ōkii desu.

Tokyo is the largest among Tokyo, Osaka and Kyoto.

no naka de is sometimes shortened to **de**.

5. Questions and Answers about comparison among more than two items.

1) Question

$$\boxed{N_1 \text{ to } N_2 \text{ to } N_3 \text{ to, } \begin{Bmatrix} \text{dore} \\ \text{doko} \\ \text{dare} \\ \text{itsu} \end{Bmatrix} \text{ ga ichiban } \begin{Bmatrix} A \\ Na \end{Bmatrix} \text{ desu ka.}}$$

$\left.\begin{matrix} Which \\ Where \\ Who \\ When \end{matrix}\right\}$ *is the most* $\begin{Bmatrix} A \\ Na \end{Bmatrix}$, *$N_1$, N_2 or N_3?*

Fune to hikōki to densha to, <u>dore</u> ga ichiban hayai desu ka.

Which is the fastest, a ship, an airplane or a train?

Tōkyō to Ōsaka to Kyōto to, <u>doko</u> ga ichiban ōkii desu ka.

Which is the largest, Tokyo, Osaka or Kyoto?

Slamet-san to Tanom-san to Rao-san to, <u>dare</u> ga ichiban wakai desu ka.

Who is the youngest, Mr. Slamet, Mr. Tanom or Mr. Rao?

Kin-yōbi to Do-yōbi to Nichi-yōbi to, <u>itsu</u> ga ichiban isogashii desu ka.

On which day are you the busiest, Friday, Saturday or Sunday?

2) Answer

$$\boxed{N_1 \text{ ga ichiban } \begin{Bmatrix} A \\ Na \end{Bmatrix} \text{ desu}}$$ *N_1 is the most* $\begin{Bmatrix} A \\ Na \end{Bmatrix}$ *of all.*

Hikōki ga <u>ichiban</u> hayai desu. *An airplane is the fastest.*

Tōkyō ga ichiban ōkii desu. *Tokyo is the largest.*

Slamet-san ga ichiban wakai desu. *Mr. Slamet is the youngest.*

Kin-yōbi ga ichiban isogashii desu. *Friday is the busiest.*

6.

$$\boxed{N \text{ [no naka] de } \begin{Bmatrix} \text{nani}^* \\ \text{doko} \\ \text{dare} \\ \text{itsu} \end{Bmatrix} \text{ ga ichiban } \begin{Bmatrix} A \\ Na \end{Bmatrix} \text{ desu ka.}}$$

$\left.\begin{matrix} Which \\ Which\ place \\ Who \\ When \end{matrix}\right\}$ *is the most* $\begin{Bmatrix} A \\ Na \end{Bmatrix}$ *among N?*

Supōtsu [no naka] de <u>nani</u> ga ichiban suki desu ka.

What do you like best among the sports?

Sekai no kuni [no naka] de <u>doko</u> ga ichiban ōkii desu ka.

What country is the largest in the World?

Kenshūsei [no naka] de <u>dare</u> ga ichiban wakai desu ka.

Who is the youngest among the trainees?

Ichi-nen [no naka] de <u>itsu</u> ga ichiban suki desu ka.

Which season (or month) do you like best in a year?

<u>※</u>
nani

When we compare things, **dore** or **nani** is used.

1. In case of choosing one thing out of the whole group, such as fruits, animal or sport, **nani** is used.

    Kudamono no naka de <u>nani</u> ga ichiban suki desu ka.

    What do you like best among fruit?

2. In case of choosing one out of the specific number of the group, such as fruit on the table, etc, **dore** is used.

    Hako no naka no kudamono no naka de <u>dore</u> ga ichiban suki desu ka.

    Which do you like best among the fruits in a box?

7. Inflection of **desu** with a noun or **na**-adjective

	non-past (present and/or future)		past	
affirmative	ame N shizuka Na }	desu	ame shizuka }	deshita
negative	ame shizuka }	dewa arimasen	ame shizuka }	dewa arimasen deshita

The *non-past* form **desu** is used for both present and future, just as the *non-past* form **-masu** is. Remember that the present-future distinction is not indicated by verb inflections in Japanese.

Kyō wa getsu-yōbi desu.　*Today is Monday.*

Ashita wa ka-yōbi desu.　*Tomorrow is Tuesday.*

8. Inflection of **i**-adjective

	non-past (present and/or future)	past
affirmative	atsui desu	atsukatta desu
negative	atsukunai desu	atsukunakatta desu

Dai 13 ka

1.

> (Watashi wa) N **ga** hoshii desu   *(I)* want N.

The particle **ga** rather than the particle **o** (as an English-speaker might expect) is used with **hoshii desu**, because **hoshii** is an i-adjective. (Lesson 9-1)

Watashi wa kamera <u>ga</u> hoshii desu.   *I want a camera.*

2.

> (watashi wa) N $\left\{ \begin{matrix} \mathbf{o} \\ \mathbf{ga} \end{matrix} \right\}$ V-**tai desu**   *(I)* want to do ...

-tai is attached to the **masu**-form of the verb, after removing **-masu**. The inflection of **-tai** is the same as other i-adjectives.

Notice that when the verb is a transitive and is preceeded by N **o** (object), this N **o** very often changes to N **ga.** This change is caused presumably because of the adjective quality of **-tai**.

Kōhii $\left\{ \begin{matrix} \mathbf{o} \\ \mathbf{ga} \end{matrix} \right\}$ **nomitai desu.**   *I want to drink coffee.*

3.

> $\left. \begin{matrix} \text{*N (of action)} \\ \text{V-[ma̶su]} \end{matrix} \right\}$ **ni** $\left\{ \begin{matrix} \text{ikimasu} \\ \text{kimasu} \\ \text{kaerimasu} \end{matrix} \right.$ *(I)* $\left\{ \begin{matrix} go \\ come \\ return \end{matrix} \right\}$ $\left\{ \begin{matrix} . \\ for ... \\ in\ order\ to ... \end{matrix} \right.$

    * Nouns of actions are a special class of nouns which refer to action. (See Lesson 14-1)

In the above construction, N **ni** or V **ni** expresses purpose.

Ōsaka e ikimasu.	*I (will) go to Osaka.*
Ōsaka e <u>jisshū</u> <u>ni</u> ikimasu. <small>N</small>	*I (will) go to Osaka for practical training.*
Eiga o mimasu.	*I (will) see a movie.*
Ginza e eiga o <u>mi</u> <u>ni</u> ikimasu. <small>V</small>	*I (will) go to Ginza to see movies.*

Notice that a verb following **...ni** (in the above pattern) is usually limited to three verbs given above, or to those which have similar meanings involving movement from place to place. If any other verb follows, purpose is expressed in the form N **no tame ni** or V-dictionary form+**tame ni**, rather than in the form N **ni** or V **ni**.

4.

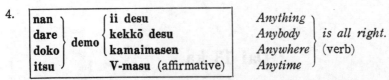

nan			ii desu		Anything	
dare	}	demo	kekkō desu		Anybody	} is all right.
doko			kamaimasen		Anywhere	(verb)
itsu			V-masu (affirmative)		Anytime	

The phrases formed by a combination of *an interrogative noun*+**demo** may be translated into English as *no matter*+(*an English interrogative noun*).

    nan demo   *no matter what* (or *anything at all*)

    dare demo   *no matter who* (or *anybody at all*)

    doko demo   *no matter where* (or *anywhere at all*)

Other verbs can be used in the pattern shown with **demo** in addition to **ii desu**, **kekkō desu**, or **kamaimasen**.

The following expressions are also used.

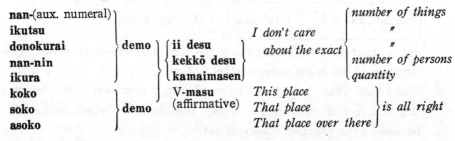

nan-(aux. numeral)							*number of things*
ikutsu			**ii desu**		*I don't care*		*"*
donokurai	}	demo	{ **kekkō desu** }		*about the exact*	{	*"*
nan-nin			**kamaimasen**				*number of persons*
ikura							*quantity*
koko			**V-masu**		*This place*		
soko	}	demo	(affirmative)		*That place*	}	*is all right*
asoko					*That place over there*		

— 34 —

Dai 14 ka

1. <u>Groups of verbs</u>

   There are three groups in Japanese verbs.

   1) I-group verbs (consonant verbs)

      This group of verbs is called *consonant verbs* because the stem ends with a consonant.

   2) II-group verbs (vowel verbs)

      This group is called *vowel verbs* because the stem ends in a vowel.

      As can be seen from the chart on the next page, the division into consonant and vowel verbs is necessary because the endings occurring after a consonant are different from those occuring after a vowel.

   3) III-group verbs (irregular verbs)

      This group is that of irregular inflection.

      Only two verbs belong to this group. There are **kimasu** *come* and **shimasu** *do*.

      However, there are also some nouns of action which change into verbs by attaching **-shimasu** to them.

benkyō (noun)	*study*
benkyō-shimasu (verb)	*to study*

2. Inflection of verbs

	I-group verbs			II-group verbs						III-group verbs					
	kakimasu *write*			tabemasu *eat*			okimasu *get up*			kimasu *come*			shimasu *do*		
	verb (stem /)		kōzoku-ku *3	verb (stem /)		kōzoku-ku	verb (stem /)		kōzoku-ku	verb (stem /)		kōzoku-ku	verb (stem /)		kōzoku-ku
a	kak	a	nai de kudasai (See L. 17) *Please don't write.*	tabe		nai de kudasai *Please don't eat.*	oki		nai de kudasai *Please don't get up.*	k	o	nai de kudasai *Please don't come.*	sh	i	nai de kudasai *Please don't do.*
i	kak	i	tai desu *I want to write.*	tabe		tai desu *I want to eat.*	oki		tai desu *I want to get up.*	k	i	tai desu *I want to come.*	sh	i	tai desu *I want to do.*
u	kak	u	koto ga dekimasu (See Lesson 18) *I can write.*	tabe	ru	koto ga dekimasu *I can eat.*	oki	ru	koto ga dekimasu *I can get up.*	k	u ru	koto ga dekimasu *I can come.*	s	u ru	koto ga dekimasu *I can do.*
*1 e	kak	e	ba *If I write, ...*	tabe	re	ba *If I eat, ...*	oki	re	ba *If I get up, ...*	k	u re	ba *If I come, ...*	s	u re	ba *If I do, ...*
*2 o	kak	o	*Let's write.*	tabe	yo	*Let's eat.*	oki	yo	*Let's get up.*	k	o yo	*Let's come.*	sh	i yo	*Let's do.*

*1, *2 ... These two forms of a verb are not treated in this book, but they are listed in Appendix 2.

*1 **kakeba, tabereba** etc.

This is a conditional form which means *if ...*; it has almost the same meaning as **V-tara** in Lesson 25.

*2 **ikō, tabeyō** etc.

This is a volitional form which means *Let's ...* or *I will ....* This is the plain volitional form. The polite volitional form is **V-mashō**.

*3 **kōzoku-ku**: This is a term for a grammatical ending to a verb or a phrase following a verb.

3. **te**-form (**te-kei**) of verbs

Besides those shown in the list, there are forms called **te**-form and **ta**-form. The **ta**-form is treated in Lesson 19.

4. How to make **te**-form (See NIHON-GO NO KISO, Lesson 14 **Renshū** A, P. 84)

II-group verb

tabe-masu	⟶	**tabe-te**	*eat*
oshie-masu	⟶	**oshie-te**	*teach*
mi-masu	⟶	**mi-te**	*see*
oki-masu	⟶	**oki-te**	*get up*

III-group verb

ki-masu	⟶	**ki-te**	*come*
shi-masu	⟶	**shi-te**	*do*

I-group verb

kaki-masu	⟶	(**kaki-te**)	⟶	**kai-te**	*write*
kiki-masu	⟶	(**kiki-te**)	⟶	**kii-te**	*hear*
(exception)					
iki-masu	⟶	(**iki-te**)	⟶	**it-te**	*go*
isogi-masu	⟶	(**isogi-te**)	⟶	**isoi-de**	*hurry*
nomi-masu	⟶	(**nomi-te**)	⟶	**non-de**	*drink*
yomi-masu	⟶	(**yomi-te**)	⟶	**yon-de**	*read*
yobi-masu	⟶	(**yobi-te**)	⟶	**yon-de**	*call*
furi-masu	⟶	(**furi-te**)	⟶	**fut-te**	*rain*
kaeri-masu	⟶	(**kaeri-te**)	⟶	**kaet-te**	*return*
ari-masu	⟶	(**ari-te**)	⟶	**at-te**	*have, exist*
machi-masu	⟶	(**machi-te**)	⟶	**mat-te**	*wait*
tachi-masu	⟶	(**tachi-te**)	⟶	**tat-te**	*stand up*
kai-masu	⟶	(**kai-te**)	⟶	**kat-te**	*buy*
sui-masu	⟶	(**sui-te**)	⟶	**sut-te**	*smoke*
ii-masu	⟶	(**ii-te**)	⟶	**it-te**	*say*
hanashi-masu		⟶		**hanashi-te**	*speak*
kashi-masu		⟶		**kashi-te**	*lend*

5. Use of **te**-form ... I

> **V-te kudasai**   *Please do ... for me.*

In a pattern of the form N **o kudasai, kudasai** means *give me* ... (Lesson 2), whereas in the pattern V-**te kudasai, kudasai** does not mean *give me* ... but means *Please do ... for me.*

That is, this pattern expresses a polite request.

    Tabete kudasai.   *Please eat.*

    Kite kudasai.   *Please come.*

    Itte kudasai.   *Please go, Please say.*

6. Use of **te**-form ... 2—A

> **V-te imasu**   *be ... ing* (progression)

This pattern expresses the idea that an action is now going on.

    Rao-san wa ima hon o yonde imasu.

    Mr. Rao is reading a book now.

7. **V-mashō** ... 2

Besides the meaning of *Let's do* ... (Lesson 6), this means *I will do* ...
V-mashō ka? means *Shall I do* ...?

    Mō ichido iimashō ka.   *Shall I say it again?*

    Hai, itte kudasai.   *Yes, please say it again.*

— 38 —

Dai 15 ka

1. Use of **te**-form ... 3

   | V-**te mo ii desu** | *It is all right if (one) does (something).*

   Tabako o sutte mo ii desu. *You may smoke.*

   The questions and answers to this pattern are as follows.

   Denki o tsukete mo ii desu ka. *May I swich on the light?*

   Hai, ii desu. (or **Hai, kekkō desu**) *Yes, you may.*

   Iie, ikemasen. (or **Iie, dame desu**) *No, you must not.*

2. Use of **te**-form ... 2—B

   | V-**te imasu** | *be ... ing*

   Besides the usage of **te**-form ... 2—A (Lesson 14), it expresses a state or a habit. The pattern above has the meaning that *the result of the action exists or the state resulting from an action exists.*

   Tanaka-san wa ii kamera o motte imasu.

   Mr. Tanaka has a nice camera.

   Watashi wa Tōkyō ni* sunde imasu.

   I live in Tokyo.

   Uketsuke de kitte o utte imasu.

   They sell postage stamps at the information desk.

   ni*   N (place) **ni** {**sunde imasu** / **imasu**}

   Particle **ni** is used with **sunde imasu** or **imasu** *live* in order to mark the noun indicating a place.

3. **shirimasen** (the negative of **shitte imasu**)

   The negative of **shitte imasu** is **shirimasen**.

   Notice that **shitte imasen** is not used.

   Rao-san o shitte imasu ka. *Do you know Mr. Rao?*

   Hai, shitte imasu. *Yes, I know him.*

   Iie, shirimasen. *No, I don't know him.*

4. ... **narimasu**

   | N \ / Na } **ni** } **narimasu** / A-**ku** | *become ...*

— 39 —

This expresses the result of some change or transformation.

      Watashi wa sensei desu.   *I am a teacher.*
             N
             ↓

      Watashi wa sensei ni narimasu.   *I will become a teacher.*

      Shizuka desu.   *(It) is quiet.*
        Na
        ↓

      Shizuka ni narimasu.   *(It) will become quiet.*

      Samui desu.   *(It) is cold.*
        A
        ↓

      Samuku narimasu.   *(It) is becoming cold.*

Na-**ni** and A-**ku** may be regarded as adverbial forms of adjectives. (See Lesson 30)

      shizuka ni *quietly*   **hayaku** *rapidly*

5. | sentence | **yo**

The final particle **yo**, which occurs at the end of a sentence, has the effect of making the sentence very assertive and positive.

      Suzuki-san desu yo.   *She is Mrs. Suzuki!*

Dai 16 ka

1. Joining more than two predicates

   1) Use of **te**-form ... 4

      | ... V-**te**, ... | *do ... , and ...* |
      | | *did ... , and ...* (successive actions or events) |

      te-form is not inflected for tense.

      Ashita Ginza e <u>itte</u>, tomodachi ni <u>atte</u>, kaimono-shimasu.

      Tomorrow, I will go to Ginza, see my friend and do some shopping.

      Kinō Ginza e <u>itte</u>, tomodachi ni <u>atte</u>, kaimono-shimashita.

      Yesterday, I went to Ginza, saw my friend and did some shopping.

   2) **te**-form of i-adjective

      | ... A-**kute**, ... | *to be ... , and ...* |

      te-form of i-adjective is A-**kute**.

      ōki-i ⟶ **ōki-kute**

      chiisa-i ⟶ **chiisa-kute**

      i-i
      yo-i } ⟶ **yo-kute**

      Kono heya wa <u>semakute</u>, kurai desu.

      This room is small and dark.

   3) **te**-form of copula **desu**

      | ... N | |
      | ... Na } **de**, ... | *to be ... , and ...* |

      The **te**-form of **desu** is **de**.

      Rao-san wa Indo-jin <u>de</u>, Ōsaka-kagaku no kenshūsei desu.

      Mr. Rao is an Indian, and he is a trainee of Ōsaka-kagaku.

      Arora-san wa kirei <u>de</u>, atama ga ii desu.

      Miss Arora is pretty ana intelligent.

2. Use of **te**-form...5

> ...V-te kara...   *after doing...,...*

V-masu. Sorekara...=V-te, sorekara...=V-te kara...

Benkyō ga <u>owarimasu</u>. Sorekara eiga o mimasu.

=Benkyō ga <u>owatte, sorekara</u> eiga o mimasu.

=Benkyō ga <u>owatte kara,</u> eiga o mimasu.

> *After studying, I will see a movie.*

Notice that **kara** comes at the end of the clause.

3. > N ga irimasu   *(I) need...*

irimasu takes particle **ga** instead of **o** to mark the noun indicating a thing which is needed.

O-kane <u>ga</u> irimasu.   *I need some money.* (Lesson 9, 1)

Dai 17 ka

1. Plain non-past negative form of verbs

   $\boxed{\text{V-nai (nai-form (nai-kei))}}$ *(I) do not...*

   V-nai is the plain-form of **V-masen.** (See Lesson 20)

2. Use of **nai**-form ... 1

   $\boxed{\text{V-nai de kudasai}}$ *Please do not...* (polite negative request)

   cf. **V-te kudasai**   *Please do...* (polite request) (Lesson 14)

   Watashi o wasurenai de kudasai.   *Please don't forget me.*

3. Use of **nai**-form ... 2

   $\boxed{\text{V-nakereba narimasen}}$ *(I) must...* (obligation)

   Literally, this pattern means *If (I) do not..., (it) is not good.*

   Watashi wa ikanakereba narimasen.   *I must go.*

4. Use of **nai**-form ... 3

   $\boxed{\text{V-nakute mo ii desu}}$ *(I) need not...* or *(I) don't have to...*

   Literally, this pattern means *Even if (I) do not..., (it) is all right.*
   The meaning is opposite that of the **V-nakereba narimasen.**

   Anata wa ikanakute mo ii desu.   *You need not go.*

                                                 You don't have to go.

5. How to make **nai**-form

   (See NIHON-GO NO KISO Lesson 17, **Renshū** A. p. 102)

   1) I group verbs

   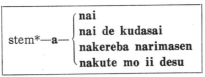

   * The stem of the I group verbs is found by deleting **i** immediately
   preceding **-masu.** (See Lesson 8)

   kak— i —masu

   kak— a — { nai / nai de kudasai / nakereba narimasen / nakute mo ii desu }

— 43 —

(Exceptions)

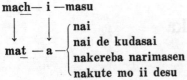

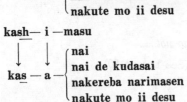

2) II group verbs

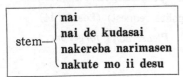

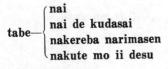

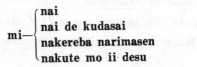

3) III group verbs

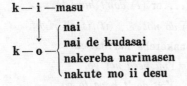

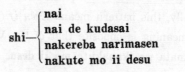

Dai 18 ka

1. Plain non-past affirmative form of verbs (dictionary form of verbs)

   | V-(r)u (dictionary form (jisho-kei)) |

   The plain non-past affirmative form or *dictionary form* is the basic form of a verb which is listed in dictionary. This form is used as the plain equivalent to **V-masu**. (See Lesson 20)

2. How to make dictionary form

   (See NIHONGO NO KISO Lesson 18. **Renshū** A, p. 108)

   1) I group verbs

      | stem—**u** |

      kak— i —masu
      ↓
      kak—**u**

      (Exceptions)

      mach— i —masu   kash— i —masu
      ↓ ↓   ↓   ↓
      mats—**u**   kas—**u**

   2) II group verbs

      | stem—**ru** |

      tabe—masu
      ↓
      tabe— ru

      mi—masu
      ↓
      mi— ru

   3) III group verbs

      k — i —masu   sh— i —masu
      ↓ ↓   ↓ ↓ ↓
      k —u— ru   s —u— ru

3. Use of dictionary form...1

   It is possible to do...
   (I) can do...

   The subject of **dekimasu** *be possible* is always a noun or a noun phrase. Sometimes the noun is a noun which refers to an action, such as **unten** *driving* as below:

   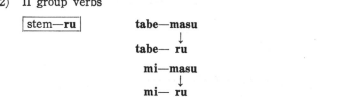

   But a noun phrase can also be the subject of **dekimasu**. Such a noun phrase

may be formed by the dictionary form of the verb (eg. **oyogu** *swim*) + koto
The resulting phrase, **oyogu koto**, may be translated into English as *swimming*. This type of phrase may then be followed by the particle **ga** as the subject of **dekimasu**, as in the following.

Watashi wa oyogu koto ga dekimasu.
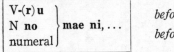

As for me, swimming is possible or a smoother variety in English, *I can swim.*

4. Meaning of **dekimasu**

dekimasu has two meanings.

1) Some action is permitted or possible in a certain place. (See NIHONGO NO KISO Lesson 18 **Renshū** B—1 p. 109)

    Uketsuke de kitte o kau koto ga dekimasu.

        I can buy postage stamps at the information desk. or *Buying postage stamps at the information desk is possible.*

2) One has the ability to do something. (See NIHONGO NO KISO Lesson 18 **Renshū**-B-2 p. 109)

    Watashi wa kanji o yomu koto ga dekimasu.

        I can read kanji. or *For me, reading kanji is possible.*

5. Use of dictionary form...2

V-(r)u N no numeral } mae ni,...	*before doing...,...* *before...,...*

A time modifier consisting of the non-past, the plain form of a verb (*i. e* the dictionary form of the verb) + **mae ni** *before* is not influenced by tense; that is, it is used both in future and past sentences.

    Kinō hiru-gohan o taberu mae ni, Nihon-go o benkyō-shimashita.
                           V

    Yesterday, I studied Japanese before I ate lunch.

    Ashita hiru-gohan o taberu mae ni, Nihon-go o benkyō-shimasu.
                           V

    Tomorrow, I will study Japanese before I eat lunch.

Notice that **mae ni** comes at the end of the clause and the non-past form **taberu** *eat* is used in both past and non-past sentences.

Hiru-gohan no mae ni, Nihon-go o benkyō-shimashita.
      N

Before lunch, I studied Japanese.

2-nen mae ni Nihon-go o benkyō-shimashita.
numeral

Two years ago, I studied Japanese.

Dai 19 ka

1. Plain past affirmative form of the verb

   | **V-ta** (ta-form (ta-kei)) |

   This is the plain form of **V-mashita**. (See Lesson 20)

2. How to make ta-form.

   This form is made by changing the final **e** of the **te**-form into **a**.

te-form		ta-form
kait-e	———————	kait-a
tabet-e	———————	tabet-a
kit-e	———————	kit-a
shit-e	———————	shit-a

3. Use of ta-form...1

   | **V-ta koto ga arimasu** | (*I*) *have had the experience of...ing*

   This pattern means that one has the experience of doing such-and-such
   action or activity.

   Anata wa Hokkaidō e itta koto ga arimasu ka.

   Have you ever been to Hokkaido?

   Hai, (itta koto ga) arimasu.

   Yes, I have been there.

   Iie, (itta koto ga) arimasen.

   No, I haven't been there.

4. Use of ta-form...2

   | **V-ta*** / **V-nai** } **hō ga ii desu** | (*You*) *had better do (such-and-such)...*
                                                       (*You*) *had better not do (such-and-such)...*

   (**Anata wa**) <u>itta</u> **hō ga ii desu.**   *You had better go.*

   (**Anata wa**) <u>ikanai</u> **hō ga ii desu.**   *You had better not go.*

   V-ta* hō ga ii desu

   V-(r)u hō ga ii desu is sometimes used instead of **V-ta hō ga ii desu.**

— 48 —

5. Use of **ta**-form . . . 3

| V-ta
N **no** } **ato de,** . . .
Numeral | *after* (*I*) *do* (*such-and-such*), ...
after (N), ...
in (Numeral), ... |

V-ta ato de has approximately the same meaning as **V-te kara.** (Lesson 16)

Hiru-gohan o tabeta ato de, Ginza e ikimasen ka.
　　　　　　　　V

Won't you go to Ginza, after you have eaten lunch ?

Hiru-gohan no ato de, Ginza e ikimasen ka.
　　　　　N

Won't you go to Ginza after lunch ?

1-jikan ato de, Ginza e ikimasen ka.
Numeral

Won't you go to Ginza in one hour ?

Dai 20 ka

1. Different levels of politeness in Japanese

   So far this text has introduced various forms which may occur at the end of a sentence as the predicate of the sentence : there are verbs (eg. **kaki masu** *write*), adjectives of two kinds (eg. **okii desu** *is big* and **kirei desu** *is-beautiful*) and the copula with a noun (eg. **Nihon-jin desu.** *is a Japanese*). These are the polite forms of predicates, and when sentences end with polite predicates, the sentences are said to be in the *polite style* (**teinei-tai**).

   In a dictionary, however, predicates are not listed in their polite forms, but rather in their plain forms. The plain form may be regarded as a *basic form* of verbs and adjectives. It is the plain form which is used in non-final positions in the sentence, as follows :

tabenai de kudasai.	(Lesson 17)
taberu mae ni, ikimasu.	(Lesson 18)
tabeta koto ga arimasu.	(Lesson 19)

   In daily intimate speech, these plain forms may also occur as sentence-final predicates in a sentence. A speech style using plain final predicates is called the *plain style* (**futsu-tai**). The *plain style* is used when speaking to a close friend. (or an inferior*.)

   * It is difficult to specify exactly the conditions under which each style may be used, since an inferior may use the plain style even with a superior if he has a close social or emotional relationship with that superior. Conversely, a superior may use the polite form even when speaking to an inferior, if he does not have a close social or intimate relationship with the inferior.

2. Two styles of the sentence.

	polite-style	plain-style	meaning
verb	**Tegami o kakimasu**	**Tegami o kaku.**	(*I*) *write a letter*
i-adj.	**Kono heya wa ōkii desu.**	**Kono heya wa ōkii.**	*This room is big.*
na-adj.	**Kono hana wa kirei desu.**	**Kono hana wa kirei da.**	*This flower is beautiful.*
noun	**Kore wa hon desu.**	**Kore wa hon da.**	*This is a book.*

3. Questions in plain style

Question particle **ka** is often omitted in a question in the plain style, in such case as the last word of the sentence has a rising intonation.

	polite-style	plain-style
verb	kakimasu ka?	kaku?
i-adj.	ōkii desu ka?	ōkii?
na-adj.	kirei desu ka?	kirei?
noun	hon desu ka?	hon?

Notice that **da** (the plain non-past form of the copula) is not used after nouns and **na**-adjectives in questions in the plain style.

Kirei desu ka? = Kirei da ?
Hon desu ka = Hon da ?

4. Plain-style of the following phrase (Conjugation patterns; **kōzoku-ku**)
   (See Lesson 29)

polite style	plain style	meaning	Lesson number
nomitai desu	**nomitai**	(I) (You)} *want to drink*	13
nomitakunai desu	**nomitakunai**	(I) (You)} *do not want to drink*	
nomi ni ikimasu	**nomi ni iku**	*go to drink*	13
nomi ni ikimasen	**nomi ni ikanai**	*not go to drink*	
o-nomi ni narimasu	**o-nomi ni naru**	*He* *You*} *drink(s)*	27
o-nomi ni narimasen	**o-nomi ni naranai**	*do(es) not drink*	
kaite kudasai	**kaite kure**[*1]	*Please write*	14
kakanai de kudasai	**kakanai de kure**	*Please do not write*	
kaite imasu	**kaite iru**	*be writing*	14
kaite imasen	**kaite inai**	*not be writing*	
kaite mo ii desu	**kaite mo ii**	*may write*	15
kakanakute mo ii desu	**kakanakute mo ii**	*does not have to write*	
kaite agemasu	**kaite ageru**	(I) *write for* {*him* *you*	27
kaite agemasen	**kaite agenai**	(I) *do not write for* {*him* *you*	
kaite kudasaimasu	**kaite kureru**[*2]	*He* *You*} *write(s) for me*	27
kaite kudasaimasen	**kaite kurenai**	*do(es) not write for me*	
kaite moraimasu	**kaite morau**	*ask (somebody) to write, and (he) writes*	27
kaite moraimasen	**kaite morawanai**	*ask (somebody) not to write, and (he) doesn't write*	
ikanakereba narimasen	**ikanakereba naranai**}	*must go*	17
ikanai to ikemasen	**ikanai to ikenai**		
itte wa ikemasen	**itte wa ikenai**	*must not go*	
taberu koto ga dekimasu	**taberu koto ga dekiru**	*can eat*	18
taberu koto ga dekimasen	**taberu koto ga dekinai**	*can not eat*	
taberu koto ga suki desu	**taberu koto ge suki da**	*like to eat*	24
taberu koto ga suki dewa arimasen	**taberu koto ga suki dewa nai**	*do(es) not like to eat*	
yonda koto ga arimasu	**yonda koto ga aru**	*have read*	19
yonda koto ga arimasen	**yonda koto ga nai**	*have never read*	
yonda hō ga ii desu	**yonda hō ga ii**	*had better read*	19
yomanai hō ga ii desu	**yomanai hō ga ii**	*had better not read*	
yomu deshō	**yomu darō**[*3]	*will probably read*	21
yomanai deshō	**yomanai darō**	*will probably not read*	
yomu kamo shiremasen	**yomu kamo shirenai**	*might read*	21
yomanai kamo shiremasen	**yomanai kamo shirenai**	*might not read*	

[*1], [*2], [*3] These patterns are not treated in this text.

5. Plain style in complex sentences

Basu wa <u>osoi desu</u> **kara, densha de** <u>ikimasu</u>. (polite style)

Basu wa <u>osoi</u> **kara, densha de** <u>iku</u>. (plain style)

The bus is slow, so (I) will go by train.

Ame ga <u>furimasu</u> **kara,** <u>dekakemasen</u>.

Ame ga <u>furu</u> **kara,** <u>dekakenai</u>.

It is going to rain, so (I) will not go out.

6. Plain form of **hai, iie**

hai ⟶ un

$$\text{iie} \longrightarrow \begin{cases} \textbf{uun} \text{ (the accent is } \underline{u}\overline{u}\underline{n}) \\ \textbf{iya} \text{ or } \textbf{iiya} \text{ (the accent is } i|\overline{ya}, \text{ ii}|\overline{ya} \end{cases}$$

7. Distinctions between speeches of males and females in use of plain style.

In a plain style sentence, there are some differences between a speech of male and that of female. The conversation in Lesson 20 is one between two men. The following is one between two women.

(Mrs. or Miss) **Toshiko** : **Genki ?**

(Mrs. or Miss) **Haruko** : **Ē, genki** <u>yo</u>.

Anata wa dō ?

Toshiko : **Watashi mo genki** <u>yo</u>.

Anata wa ashita doko e iku <u>no</u> ?

Haruko : **Doko mo ikanai** <u>wa</u> [<u>yo</u>].

Toshiko : **Jā,** <u>watashi</u> **to issho ni Kyōto e ikanai ?**

Haruko : **Sore wa ii** <u>wa</u> **ne.**

Dai 21 ka

1. ...to omoimasu

Sentence in the plain style (futsū-tai)	to omoimasu

(I) think that...,
(I) suppose...,
(I) guess...

Kare wa ashita kaisha e iku to omoimasu.

I think he will go to the company tomorrow.

Kare wa ashita kaisha e ikanai to omoimasu.

I don't think he will go to the company tomorrow.

Kare wa kinō kaisha e itta to omoimasu.

I think he went to the company yesterday.

Kare wa kinō kaisha e ikanakatta to omoimasu.

I don't think he went to the company yesterday.

2. ...to iimasu

Sentence in the plain style (futsū-tai)	
Sentence in the polite style (teinei-tai)	to iimasu

{(He) says that...
People say that...}
He says "..."

In Japanese, the difference between direct and indirect quotations is not so remarkable as in English.

Tanom-san wa Ginza e iku to iimashita.

Mr. Tanom said that he would go to Ginza.

Tanom-san wa "Ginza e ikimasu." to iimashita.

Mr. Tanom said "I will go to Ginza."

3. Particle to...3

This means *that...*

...**to** omoimasu	*I think that...*
...**to** iimasu	*I say that...*

— 54 —

4. List of ...**to omoimasu** and ...**to iimasu**

plain form of V		
...(r)u		iku
...nai		ikanai
...ta		itta
...nakatta		ikanakatta
plain form of A		
...i		samui
...kunai	to omoimasu	samukunai
...katta	to iimasu	samukatta
...kunakatta		samukunakatta
N		
Na		
...da		Nihon-jin / kirei } da
...dewa nai		Nihon-jin / kirei } dewa nai
...datta		Nihon-jin / kirei } datta
...dewa nakatta		Nihon-jin / kirei } dewa nakatta

} to omoi-masu / to ii-masu

5. Omission of **to**

When **omoimasu** or **iimasu** is used with such a word as **sō** *so* or **dō** *how*, particle **to** is omitted.

Sō { omoimasu. — *I think so.*
{ iimasu. — *I Say so.*

Dō { omoimasu ka. — *How do you think?*
{ iimasu ka. — *How do you say?*

6. **sonnani**... negative.

| sonnani A-ku nai |

| sonnani Na dewa nai | *not so...*

sonnani, when used with a negative, has the meaning *not so...* or *not very...*, just like **amari** with negative. (Lesson 8)

Kyō wa sonnani atsuku nai desu *It is not so hot today.*

Koko wa sonnani shizuka dewa *This place is not so quiet.*
arimasen.

7. Use of **deshō** ... 1 ;   **kamo shiremasen**

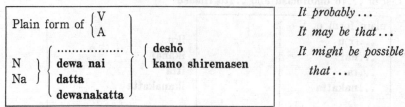

The lack of certainty expressed by **deshō** may be expressed in English with various of devices, such as *I suppose ...*, *probably ...*, *etc.* The form **deshō** is used in statements referring to past as well as non-past matters.

> **Ali-san wa raishū kuni e kaeru deshō.**
>> *Mr. Ali will probably go back to his country next week.*

> **Ali-san wa senshū kuni e kaetta deshō.**
>> *Mr. Ali went back to his country last week, I suppose.*

> **Ali-san wa raishū kuni e kaeru kamo shiremasen.**
>> *It may be that Mr. Ali will go back to his country next week.*

> **Ali-san wa senshū kuni e kaetta kamo shiremasen.**
>> *It may be that Mr. Ali went back to his country last week.*

8. Pronunciation of **deshō** and **desu yo**

deshō and **desu yo** (**Nihongo no Kiso** Lesson 15, **Kaiwa,** p. 88) are often confused by foreigners, because the sounds are similar. In **desu yo, o** of **yo** is a short vowel.

> **Ano hito wa kenshūsei deshō.**   *He is probably a trainee.*
> **Ano hito wa kenshūsei desu yo.**   *He is a trainee.* (strong conclusion)

9. Difference between **deshō** and **kamo shiremasen**

The semantic difference between **deshō** and **kamo shiremasen** is in a degree of certainty. A statement which ends with **deshō** is more certain than one ending with **kamo shiremasen**. In the case of **deshō,** there is a subjective feeling that there is about 80% ~ 90% chance that the information in the sentence is correct or that the action referred to in the sentence will or did occur. In case of **kamo shiremasen,** however, the feeling is that there is only about 50% chance.

10. Use of **deshō** ... 2

deshō with a rising intonation is a question asking for a listener's agreement with a statement. (NIHONGO NO KISO, p. 124 **Kaiwa,** p. 125 **Reibun** 8, p. 128 **Renshū** 6.)

Nihon-go wa omoshiroi deshō ? *Japanese is interesting, isn't it ?*
Ē, omoshiroi desu. *Yes, it is interesting.*

Dai 22 ka

1. <u>toki</u>

N **no** Na-**na** A (plain present form) V (plain form) } **toki**, ...	*When...,...* *While...,...* (*During the time of...*)

toki connects two sentences, and is a noun grammatically.

   Kodomo <u>no</u> toki, Ōsaka ni sunde imashita.
      N

     When I was a child, I lived in Osaka.

   <u>Hima-na</u> toki, asobi ni kite kudasai.
     Na

     When you are free, please come and see me.

   <u>Isogashii</u> toki, tetsudatte kudasai.
     A

     When I am busy, please help me.

   Michi o <u>aruku</u> toki, jidosha ni chui-shimashō.
       V-dic.

     Let's be careful about cars, when (we) walk along the street.

   Ginza e <u>itta</u> toki, kono shatsu o kaimashita.
      V-ta

     When I went to Ginza, I bought this shirt.

2. Tense of adjectives in clauses with **toki**

If an adjective occurs in the clause with **toki,** it is always in the non-past form, regardless of the tense of the verb in a main clause.

   Watashi wa <u>wakai</u> toki, Tōkyō ni sunde <u>imashita</u>.
      A (non-past)   V (past)
   When I was young, I lived in Tokyo.

3. Tense of verbs in the clause with **toki**

A verb occurring in the clause with **toki** does not necessarily agree in tense with the predicate of the main clause. Tense in the **toki**-clause is chosen according to the following principles:

1) The dictionary form of verb is used when the action has not been completed by the time when the action in the main clause occurs.

   Ōsaka e <u>iku</u> toki, kono kaban o kaimashita.

When I was going to leave for Osaka, I bought this bag.

2) **ta**-form of verb is used when action of **toki**-clause has been completed by the time when the action of the main clause occurs.

      Ōsaka e itta toki, kono kaban o kaimashita.

      When I arrived at Osaka, I bought this bag.

4. Particele **to**...4

V-dictionary form V-**nai** form	**to, ...**	*When (if)..., (then consequently)....* *When (if)... not, (then consequently)....*

      Ongaku o kiku to, tanoshiku narimasu.

      When we listen to music, we feel happy.

      Yoru ni naru to, samuku narimashita.

      When night came, it became colder.

      Kono michi o massugu iku to, eki ga arimasu.

      If you go straight this way, there is a station.

      Motto benkyō-shinai to komarimasu yo.

      If you don't study harder, you will be in trouble.

5. Particle **o** ... 2

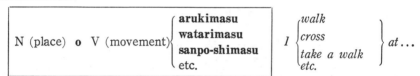

In addition to the particle **o** which marks the object of a transitive verb, there is another particle **o**. This particle occurs as a marker of the area or place through which motion occurs. A noun or noun phrase marked with this is used with some verbs expressing movement, such as **arukimasu** *walk*, **watarimasu** *cross*, **sanpo-shimasu** *take a walk*, etc.

Hashi o watarimasu.	*(I) cross the bridge.*
Kōen o sanpo-shimashō.	*Let's take a walk in the park.*
Hikōki wa sora o tobimasu.	*Airplanes fly in the sky.*
Fune wa umi o ikimasu.	*Ships sail in the sea.*

Dai 23 ka

1. Relative clauses

> (Sentence) N

In Japanese all modifiers precede what they modify. This is true whether the modifier is a word, a phrase or even a whole sentence. Note that this is very different from English, in which relative clauses follow the word they modify rather than precede it as Japanese. The function of the sentence preceding a noun in Japanese is similar to that of the relative clause following a noun in English, but (1) the positions in each case are different with respect to the modified noun, and (2) there are no relative pronouns in Japanese. The verb in a modifying sentence which precedes a noun in Japanese usually occurs in the plain rather than the polite form.

kōjō (N)	*a factory*
watashi no kōjō (N no N)	*my factory*
ōkii kōjō (A N)	*big factory*
yūmei-na kōjō (Na N)	*famous factory*
<u>**Abebe-san ga jisshū-shite iru**</u> **kōjō.** (Sentence N)	*a factory in which Mr. Abebe is wokring*

2. ga as a marker of subjects in modifying sentences

The subject of the modifying sentence is usually marked by the particle **ga.**

Watashi wa kamera o kaimashita.

I bought a camera.

Watashi ga* katta kamera wa takai desu.

The camera which I bought is expensive.

* Sometimes **no** is used instead of **ga.**

3. Example sentences with relative clauses.

1) N wa ⓜN desu.	1) **Abebe-san wa <u>kinō kita</u> <u>kenshūsei</u> desu.**
	Mr. Abebe is a trainee who came yesterday.
2) ⓜN wa N desu.	2) **<u>Kinō kita</u> <u>kenshūsei</u> wa Abebe-san desu.**
	The trainee who came yesterday is Mr. Abebe.
3) ⓜN wa {A / Na} desu.	3) **<u>Kinō kita</u> <u>kenshūsei</u> wa wakai desu.**
	The trainee who came yesterday is young.
4) N wa ⓜN o V.	4) **Watashi wa <u>kinō kita</u> <u>kenshūsei</u> o shitte imasu.**
	I know the trainee who came yesterday.
5) ⓜN wa N o V.	5) **<u>Kinō kita</u> <u>kenshūsei</u> wa Nihon-go o benkyō-shite**

imasu.

The trainee who came yesterday is studying Japanese.

* ⓜ...modifier

4. **ōki-na, chiisa-na**

   ōkii and **chiisai** are **i**-adjectives, but they may end either with **i** or **na** before a noun. In the negative, only **-ku nai desu** is used.

   ōki-i kōjō }
   ōki-na kōjō } *a large factory*

   chiisa-i kōjō }
   chiisa-na kōjō } *a small factory*

Dai 24 ka

1. Transformation of verbs into noun phrases

| V-(plain-form) **koto** |

A verb may be changed into a noun phrase by adding **koto** after the plain-form of the verb.

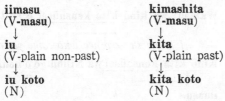

iimasu
(V-masu)
↓
iu
(V-plain non-past)
↓
iu koto
(N)

kimashita
(V-masu)
↓
kita
(V-plain past)
↓
kita koto
(N)

In Japanese, two sentences may be combined into a complex sentence by transforming one sentence into a noun phrase with the use of **koto**. This noun phrase may then replace a noun (eg. **sore**) in the second sentence.

1. **Nihon-go o hanashimasu.**   *I speak Japanese.*
2. **Sore wa muzukashii desu.**   *It is difficult.*

    Nihon-go o hanasu koto wa muzukashii desu.

      It is difficult to speak Japanese. or

      Speaking Japanese is difficult.

1. **Watashi no shumi wa kore desu.**   *My hobby is this.*
2. **E o kakimasu.**   *I paint pictures.*

    Watashi no shumi wa e o kaku koto desu.

      My hobby is painting pictures.

1. **Ano hito <u>wa</u>* kaerimashita.**   *He returned.*
2. **Sore o shitte imasu ka.**   *Do you know it?*

    Ano hito <u>ga</u>* kaetta koto o shitte imasu ka.

      Do you know that he went home?

    wa*→ga*

ga usually marks the subject of the modifying sentence.

Dai 25 ka

1. <u>Conditional form</u>

   1)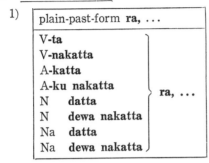

   The conditional form is made by attaching **ra** to the plain past **form.**

   Yukkuri hanashitara, wakarimasu.

   > *If you talk slowly, I understand.* or
   > *When you talk slowly, I understand.*

   Yukkuri hanasanakattara wakarimasen.

   > *If you don't talk slowly, I don't understand.*

   Yasukattara, kaimasu.

   > *If it is cheap, I will buy it.*

   Yasuku nakattara, kaimasen.

   > *If it is not cheap, I will not buy it.*

   Ame dattara, uchi ni imasu.

   > *If it rains, I will stay at home.* or
   > *When it rains, I stay at home.*

   Ame dewa nakattara, dekakemasu.

   > *If it doesn't rain, I will go out.*

   Hima dattara, tetsudatte kudasai.

   > *If you are free, please help me.*

   Hima dewa nakattara, tetsudawanakute mo ii desu.

   > *If you are not free, you need not help me.*

   2) | Interrogative+V-tara, ii desu ka | *What* |
      |---|---|
      | | *How* } *should (I) do?* |
      | | *etc.* |

   When one wants to do something but he doesn't know how to do it, **this** question pattern may be used to ask someone's advice.

   Ginkō wa dō ittara ii desu ka.　　*How should I go to the bank?*

This sentence means,

I want to go to the bank, but I don't know how to get there, so please tell me the way.

Dō ittara ii desu ka.	*Which way should I go?*
Dare to ittara ii desu ka.	*With whom should I go?*
Itsu ittara ii desu ka.	*When should I go?*
Doko e ittara ii desu ka.	*Where should I go?*

3. Concessive form...1

```
┌─────────────────────────┐
│ te-form mo, ...         │
├─────────────────────────┤
│ V-te          ┐         │
│ V-nakute      │         │
│ A-kute        │         │
│ A-ku nakute   │ mo, ... │        Even if..., ...
│ N    de       │         │
│ N    de nakute │        │
│ Na   de       │         │
│ Na   de nakute ┘        │
└─────────────────────────┘
```

The concessive form is made by attaching **mo** to **te**-form.

Ame ga futte mo, ikimasu.

Even if it rains, I will go.

Ame ga furanakute mo, ikimasen.

Even if it doesn't rain, I won't go.

Yasukute mo, kaimasen.

Even if it is cheap, I won't buy it.

Yasukunakute mo, kaimasu.

Even if it isn't cheap, I'll buy it.

Nichi-yōbi demo, hatarakimasu.

Even though it's Sunday, I work.

Nichi-yōbi de nakute mo, hatarakimasen.

Even though it's not Sunday, I don't work.

Shizuka demo, yoku neru koto ga dekimasen.

Even if it is quiet, I can't sleep well.

Shizuka dewa nakute mo, yoku neru koto ga dekimasu.

Even if it is not quiet, I can sleep well.

4. Concessive form... 2

| ikura V-te mo, ... | *However hard one may...,...*

This sentence pattern means *However hard (or, no matter how much) one does such-and-such, he can't do so-and-so. (i.e. he can't attain his goal.)*

Ikura yonde mo, kare wa kimasen.

No matter how much I may call him, he would not come.

Dai 26 ka

1. Potential Verbs

		potential form	
		polite	plain
I group verb	kakimasu hanashimasu	kakemasu hanasemasu	kakeru hanaseru
II group verb	okimasu tabemasu	okiraremasu taberaremasu	okirareru taberareru
III group verb	kimasu shimasu	koraremasu dekimasu	korareru dekiru

The potential verbs take **ga** as the object-marking particle instead of **o**.

Nihon-go o hanasu koto ga dekimasu. (Lesson 18)⎫   *I can speak*
Nihon-go ga hanasemasu.   ⎭   *Japanese.*

Kore o suru koto ga dekimasu ka. (Lesson 18)⎫
                                          Can you do this?
Kore ga dekimasu ka.   ⎭

All potential verbs are II group verbs.

2. miemasu ; kikoemasu

The intransitive verb of **mimasu** *see* is **miemasu**, and that of **kikimasu** is **kikoemasu**. **Miemasu** and **kikoemasu** implicate the potentiality, following a particle **ga**.

Watashi wa Fujisan o mimasu.   *I see Mt. Fuji.*
Fuji-san ga miemasu.   *Mt. Fuji can be seen.*
                              or Mt. Fuji is visible.

Watashi wa ongaku o kikimasu.   *I listen to the music.*
Ongaku ga kikoemasu.   *The music is audible.*

3. dekimasu

dekimasu means *can* (Lesson 18). In addition, it means *to be ready, to be completed, to be constructed, to be made*, etc.

Gohan ga dekimashita.   *Dinner is ready.*
Atarashii michi ga dekimashita.   *A new road has been constructed.*

4. **...shika...** negative

The conbination of **shika**+negative means *only*.

    100-en <u>shika arimasen.</u>   *I have ￥100 only.*

5. N (time) **made ni**

This means *not later than the time given,* **made** means that an action or a state continues till the time given, whereas **made ni** means that an action should be completed by the time.

    6-ji <u>made</u> <u>ni</u> kaerimasu.   *I'll come back <u>by</u> 6 o'clock.*

    cf. 6-ji <u>made</u> benkyō-shimasu.   *I'll study <u>till</u> 6 o'clock.*

Dai 27 ka

1. Verb meaning giving and receiving

1) N o agemasu
   N o kudasaimasu } *give something*

Both **agemasu** and **kudasaimasu** mean *give*, but there are some differences in usage.

agemasu (the original meaning is *raise*) is used when *I* (the first person) give something to *you* (the second person) or *him* (the third person).

kudasaimasu (the original meaning is *lower*) is used when *you* or *he* give something to *me*.

The particle **ni** marks a receiver.

Watashi wa { anata
              ano hito } <u>ni</u> hon o agemashita.

I gave a book to { *you.*
                     him.

Anata
ano hito } wa watashi <u>ni</u> hon o kudasaimashita.

You
He } *gave a book to me.*

cf. **Hon o kudasai.** *Please give <u>me</u> a book.*

kudasai is grammatically the imperative form of **kudasaimasu.**

The following diagram depicts the pattern of usage for the two verbs **kudasaimasu** and **agemasu.**

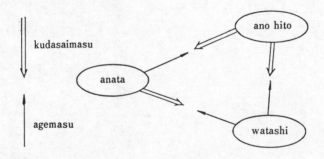

2) N o moraimasu *receive something*

moraimasu means to *receive* (Lesson 7). One of the particles **ni** or **kara** marks the giver. This particle **ni** means *from*.

— 68 —

Watashi wa $\left\{\begin{array}{l}\text{anata}\\\text{ano hito}\end{array}\right\}\left\{\begin{array}{l}\underline{\text{ni}}\\\underline{\text{kara}}\end{array}\right\}$ hon o moraimashita.

I received a book from $\left\{\begin{array}{l}you.\\him.\end{array}\right.$

2. $\boxed{\text{V-te}\left\{\begin{array}{l}\text{agemasu}\\\text{kudasaimasu}\\\text{moraimasu}\end{array}\right.}$ *do a favor of -ing for somebody.*
receive a favor of -ing from somebody.

V-te agemasu, V-te kudasaimasu do not mean *give*. They mean to do a favor of doing something for somebody. The difference between V-te agemasu and V-te kudasaimasu is the same as that between agemasu and kudasaimasu V-te moraimasu does not mean *receive*. It means *receive a favor of doing something from somebody*.

Watashi wa $\left\{\begin{array}{l}\text{anata}\\\text{ano hito}\end{array}\right\}$ ni hon o yonde agemashita.

I read a book for $\left\{\begin{array}{l}you.\\him.\end{array}\right.$

$\left.\begin{array}{l}\text{Anata}\\\text{Ano hito}\end{array}\right\}$ wa watashi ni hon o yonde kudasaimashita.

$\left.\begin{array}{l}You\\He\end{array}\right\}$ *read a book for me.*

Watashi wa anata $\left\{\begin{array}{l}\text{ni}\\\text{kara}\end{array}\right\}$ hon o yonde moraimashita.

I received $\left\{\begin{array}{l}your\\his\end{array}\right\}$ *favor of reading a book for me.*

It is difficult to choose between (V-te) agemasu and (V-te) kudasaimasu when talking about acts of giving involving the listener and a third person, or those involving two third persons. Roughly speaking in case where the listener gives something to a third person, agemasu is used, whereas in cases where a third person gives something to the listener, kudasaimasu is used. In cases where a third person gives something to another third person, both agemasu and kudasaimasu can be used. Note that kudasaimasu is not used when watashi* (the speaker) is a giver, and agemasu is not used when watashi* (the speaker) is a receiver.

* In the usage of the verbs of giving, the same principles are applied to the speaker's family or family member as to the speaker. That is when an outsider gives something to the speaker's family (or family member) agemasu is never used. Similarly, when the speaker's family (or family member) gives something to an outsider kudasaimasu is never used.

$\left.\begin{array}{l}\text{Anata}\\\text{Ano hito}\end{array}\right\}$ wa shujin ni nani o kudasaimashita ka.

What did $\begin{Bmatrix} you \\ he \end{Bmatrix}$ *give to my husband?*

Shujin wa $\begin{Bmatrix} \textbf{anata} \\ \textbf{ano hito} \end{Bmatrix}$ ni nani o agemashita ka.

What did my husband give to $\begin{Bmatrix} you? \\ him? \end{Bmatrix}$

Besides **agemasu, kudasaimasu, moraimasu**, there are some verbs of giving and receiving which are not treated in this book.

> **yarimasu** : the rough counterpart of **agemasu**
>
> **kuremasu** : the plain counterpart of **kudasaimasu**
>
> **itadakimasu**: the polite counterpart of **moraimasu**

3. | **V-te kudasaimasen ka** | *Won't you please...?*

When **-masen ka** is added to **kudasai**, the request becomes softer or more polite.

> **Matte kudasai.** *Please wait.*
>
> **Matte kudasaimasen ka.** *Won't you please wait?*

4. | o V-[m<del>asu</del>] kudasai | *Please do...*

This pattern is a more formal expression than **V-te kudasai**.

> **o machi kudasai** = **matte kudasai** *Please wait.*
>
> **o hairi kudasai** = **haitte kudasai** *Please come in.*

V-te kudasai is used with all verbs, but **o V-[m<del>asu</del>] kudasai** is not used with several verbs such as **ikimasu, kimasu, imasu, mimasu, shimasu**, etc.

5. Honorific form

Japanese language has a very polite form called **Keigo**, which shows respect. There are both a honorific form and a humble form* in keigo.

The honorific form is used when a speaker refers to a actions of a person with whom the speaker would like to cultivate a beneficial relationship. The humble form is used when a speaker refers to his own action while talking to such a person.

* The humble form is not treated in this text book.

1) | o V-[m<del>asu</del>] ni narimasu | (honorific form of V-masu)

> **Anata wa kakimasu ka.** ⇨ **Anata wa okaki ni narimasu ka.**
>
> *Will you write?*
>
> **Tanaka-san wa machimashita.** ⇨ **Tanaka-san wa omachi ni narimashita.**
>
> *Mr. Tanaka waited.*

Notice that the honorific form is not used when a speaker refers to his own action.

This honorific form is not used with the verbs as shown in the following list, since the honorific sense of these verbs is expressed by using special honorific verbs rather than honorific form of ordinary verbs shown in 5-1).

2) List of special Honorific words

		Honorific	
		polite form	plain form
ikimasu kimasu imasu	go come be, stay	irasshaimasu oide ni narimasu*	irassharu oide ni naru
tabemasu nomimasu	eat drink	meshiagarimasu	meshiagaru
iimasu	say	osshaimasu	ossharu
nemasu	sleep	o-yasumi ni narimasu	o-yasumi ni naru
mimasu	see	goran ni narimasu*	goran ni naru
shimasu	do	nasaimasu*	nasaru

* These words are not treated in this textbook.

3) Non-past polite form of **kudasaru, irassharu, ossharu, nasaru** etc.

The non-past polite form of these words are not the same as the ordinal **ra**-line verbs such as **kaerimasu** *return* **tomarimasu** *stop* etc.

dictionary-form	non-past polite form
kudasaru	**kudasaimasu** (*not* kudasarimasu)
irassharu	**irasshaimasu**
ossharu	**osshaimasu**
nasaru	**nasaimasu**

Dai 28 ka

[1] Particles

1. wa

This particle marks the subject or the topic of a sentence.

Watashi wa Lee desu.   *I am Lee.*

Tōkyō wa hito ga ōi desu.   *There are a lot of people in Tokyo.*

2. no

A : This particle follows a noun which is modifying another noun.

Kore wa watashi no hon desu.   *This is my book.*

Watashi wa Tōkyō-kikai no kenshūsei desu.

                                         I am a trainee of Tokyo-kikai.

Kore wa Nihon no tokei desu.   *This is a Japanese watch.*

Kore wa terebi no hon desu.   *This is a book on television.*

B : **No** is also sometimes used in place of a noun.

Kore wa watashi no desu.   *This is mine.*

Chiisai no o kudasai.   *Give me the small one.*

3. o

A : This particle marks the (direct) object.

Gohan o tabemasu.   *I'm going to eat (a meal).*

B : **o** may also be used to mark the separation point with certain verbs involving the idea of separation.

Heya o demasu.   *I'm going to go out of the room.*

Densha o orimasu.   *I'm going to get off the train.*

C : Finally, **o** is used to mark the area through which a motion occurs with various verbs of motions, such as **sanpo-shimasu, watarimasu, arukimasu, ikimasu,** etc.

Hashi o watarimasu.   *I walk across the bridge.*

4. | ga |

A : | N₁ wa N₂ ga { A / Na / V |

The particle **ga** in above sentence pattern, is very often used. **wa** marks the topic of a sentence and **ga** marks the subject. This subject usually shows up as the object in equivalent English sentences. See the meaning of following sentences.

Arora-san wa me ga ōkii desu.

As for Miss Arora, eyes are big.=

Miss Arora's eyes are big.=

Miss Arora has big eyes.

Examples of verbs, i-adjectives and **na**-adjectives having such **ga** marked subjects are as follows. (Lesson 9–1)

suki desu *like,* **kirai desu** *dislike,* **jōzu desu** *good at,* **wakarimasu** *understand,* **arimasu** *have,* **hoshii desu** *want,* **dekimasu** *can do,* **V-tai desu** *want to...,* **irimasu** *need*

Watashi wa kodomo ga arimasu. V	*I have children.*
Watashi wa banana ga suki desu. Na	*I like bananas.*
Watashi wa sakana ga kirai desu. Na	*I don't like fish.*
Lee-san wa pinpon ga jōzu desu. Na	*Mr. Lee is good at pingpong.*
Watashi wa dansu ga heta desu. Na	*I am poor at dancing.*
Watashi wa Nihon-go ga wakarimasu. V	*I understand Japanese.*
Watashi wa kamera ga hoshii desu. A	*I want a camera.*
Watashi wa okane ga irimasu. V	*I need money.*
Watashi wa Nihon-go ga dekimasu. V	*I can speak Japanese.*
Watashi wa eiga ga mitai desu. A	*I want to see the movies.*
Arora-san wa atama ga ii desu. A	*Miss Arora is clever.*

B :

ga is also used to mark the subject of the intransitive verb, used with **imasu** and **arimasu** (verbs of existence).

Kyōshitsu ni kenshūsei _ga_ imasu.   *There are some trainees in the classroom.*

Kyōshitsu ni tsukue _ga_ arimasu.   *There are some desks in the classroom.*

C :

1) **ga** is also used with **ichiban...** (the superative degree of comparison)

Rao-san _ga_ ichiban wakai desu.   *Mr. Rao is the youngest.*

2) **ga** is also used to mark the subject of a sentence expressing natural processes.

Ame _ga_ futte imasu.   *It is raining.*

D : There is another particle **ga** in Japanese which means *but*.

Watashi no heya wa chiisai desu _ga_, kirei desu.

     My room is small but clean.

Iroiro arimasu _ga_, donna tēpu-rekōdā ga ii desu ka.

     There are many models, and what kind of tape-recorder do you want?

E : The particle **ga** may mark the subject of subordinate clauses.

Tomodachi _ga_ kekkon-suru toki, nan to iimasu ka.

     When your friend gets married, what do you say to him?

Kore wa watashi _ga_ totta shashin desu.

     This is the photo which I took.

5. | ni |

1) The particle **ni** occurs after time expressions which indicate the time when an action occurs.

Maiasa 6-ji _ni_ okimasu.   *I get up at six every morning.*

2) Another particle **ni** marks the indirect object.

Tomodachi _ni_ tegami o kakimasu.   *I'll write a letter to my friend.*

3) With a few verbs such as **moraimasu** *receive*, **naraimasu** *learn*, a noun followed by the particle **ni** indicates the source of the thing received.

Tanaka-san _ni_ Nihon-go o naraimashita.

     I learned Japanese from Mr. Tanaka.

4) The particle **ni** may also mark the point of goal at which one will arrive. It is used with **hairimasu, aimasu, norimasu,** etc.

Tomodachi _ni_ aimasu.   *I will meet my friend.*

Ano resutoran _ni_ hairimashō.   *Let's go into that restaurant.*

Densha _ni_ norimasu.   *I get on a train.*

— 74 —

5) The particle **ni** may follow a place noun thus expressing the location where something exists. **ni** is used in this way with **arimasu, imasu, sunde imasu** etc.

> **Koko ni hon ga arimasu.** *Here is a book.*

6) The particle **ni** is used in phrases meaning the number of time or amount per unit of time, weight, etc.

> **1-shūkan ni 1-kai sentaku-shimasu.** *I wash my clothes once a week.*
> **1-nichi ni 3-jikan benkyō-shimasu.** *I study 3 hours a day.*

7) The particle **ni** may follow a phrase expressing the purpose with verbs **ikimasu, kimasu** and **kaerimasu**, etc.

> **shokudō e gohan o tabe ni ikimasu.**
> *I'm going to the dining hall to eat.*

8) The particle **ni** may also mark the result of a change of a state. Such a usage occurs with **narimasu** *become.*

> **Lee-san wa sensei ni narimashita.** *Mr. Lee became a teacher.*

6. [e]

This particle marks the noun indicating direction used with verbs of motion such as **ikimasu** *go*, **kimasu** *come*, **kaerimasu** *go back.*

> **Yokohama e(ni) ikimasu.** *I'm going to Yokohama.*

7. [de]

1) This particle marks means of transportation.

> **Hikōki de kimashita.** *I came by airplane.*

2) This particle marks the location where action occurs.

> **Niwa de shashin o torimasu.** *I take photos in the garden.*

3) This particle marks the tool, instruments or method used in performing an action.

> **Pen de tegami o kakimasu.**
> *I'm going to write a letter with a pen.*

> **Nihon-go de repōto o kakimasu.** *I write a report in Japanese.*

8. [to]

A : The particle **to** occurs after a noun, connecting it with a following noun. It may be translated as *and*.

> **Matchi to haizara wa doko desu ka.**
> *Where are matches and an ashtray?*

B : The particle **to** may also follow a noun which is in its turn followed by **issho ni**. The combination noun plus **to** plus **issho ni** may be translated as *with* (*noun*). **issho ni** can be omitted.

    Tomodachi to [issho ni] ikimasu.   *I go with my friend.*

C : The particle **to** is used after a plain style sentence, together with **omoimasu** and others having similar meanings. And this is also used after a plain or polite sentence, with **iimasu** and others having similar meanings. This may be translated as *that*. (Lesson 21)

    Ashita ame ga furu to omoimasu.   *I think it will rain tomorrow.*

    Sakamoto-san wa konban anata ni aitai to iimashita.

    Mr. Sakamoto said that he would like to see you this evening.

D : The particle **to** is used after a dictionary-form or **nai**-form of a verb, and is translated as *if...*, or *when....* V-dic. **to** and V-**nai to** are a weak conditional form. (Lesson 22)

    Ongaku o kiku to, tanoshiku narimasu.

    When we listen to music, we feel happy.

    Motto benkyō-shinai to komarimasu yo.

    If you don't study harder, you will be in trouble.

9. |ya...(nado)|

This particle occurs between nouns in a series and gives the idea that the series is not exhaustively listed. It may be translated as *... and so on.*

    Koko ni hon ya nōto ya enpitsu nado ga arimasu.

    There are books, notebooks, pencils and so on here.

10. |...kara...made|

This sequence means *from...to...*

    12-ji kara 1-ji made yasumimasu.

    I take a rest from 12 o'clock till 1 o'clock.

    Tōkyō kara Ōsaka made shinkansen de ikimasu.

    I go from Tokyo to Osaka by the Shinkansen (train).

11. |kara|

This particle indicates the reason or cause of the following clause.

    Watashi wa onaka ga itai desu kara, heya de nemasu.

    As I have a stomachache, I will go to bed in my room.

12. **ka**

   A : This particle occurs at the end of a sentence making the sentence interrogative.

         Anata wa Tanom-san desu <u>ka</u>.   *Are you Mr. Tanom?*

   B : The particle **ka** is also used (with falling intonation) at the end of a response to information given you by another speaker.

         Ano hito wa kenshūsei desu.   *He is a trainee.*

         Ā, sō desu <u>ka</u>.   *Oh, I see.*

   C : The particle **ka** may occur between two nouns, connecting them. In this case it may be translated as *or*.

         Ueno <u>ka</u> Asakusa ga ii desu.   *Ueno or Asakusa would be nice.*

13. **yori**

This particle occurs after a certain standard with which another item is compared.

         Tōkyō wa Ōsaka <u>yori</u> ōkii desu.   *Tokyo is bigger than Osaka.*

14. **mo**

   A : This particle may be translated into English as *also*, *too*, etc.

         Ano hito wa kenshūsei desu. Soshite watashi <u>mo</u> kenshūsei desu.

         He is a trainee. And I am (a trainee), too.

   B : This particle also occurs after interrogative nouns in negative sentences. In this case, it has the effect of emphasizing the negative meaning.

         Doko (e) <u>mo</u> ikimasen.   *I won't go anywhere.*

         Nani <u>mo</u> tabemasen.   *I don't eat anything.*

         Dare <u>mo</u> imasen.   *No one is here.*

15. **demo**

The form **demo** occurs after interrogative nouns in affirmative sentences. It has the effect of emphasizing the affirmative meaning.

         Nan <u>demo</u> ii desu.   *Anything is all right.*

16. **ne**

This final particle asks for the hearer's approval and is similar in function to such English structures as *isn't it?*, *aren't you?*, *doesn't he?*, *right?*, etc.

         Lee-san to onaji desu <u>ne</u>.   *It's the same as Mr. Lee isn't it?*

17. **yo**

The particle **yo** occurs at the end of a sentence and has the effect of making the sentence very assertive and positive.

    Suzuki-san desu yo.   *She is Mrs. Suzuki!*

[2] Difference between **wa** and **ga**

    it is difficult for foreigners to choose **wa** or **ga**.

1. **wa**

If an attention is focused on the predicate or if the predicate expresses new information, while the subject merely repeats old information, then **wa** rather than **ga** is used following the subject.

    Q : **Anata wa donata desu ka.**   *Who are you?*

    A : **[Watashi wa] Rao desu.**   *I am Rao.*

    Q : **Rao-san wa donata desu ka.**   *Which one is Mr. Rao?*

    A : **[Rao wa] watashi desu.**   *I am.*

In the answers, the old information (or that marked by **wa**) can be omitted.

2. **ga**

When the focus of attention is on the subject or when the subject is new information whereas the predicate is old information, then the subject is marked by **ga** rather than **wa**.

    Q : **Donata ga Rao-san desu ka.**   *Which one is Mr. Rao?*

    A : **Watashi [ga Rao] desu.**   *I am.*

In the answer, the old information can be omitted.

Notice that the sentence **Rao ga watashi desu** is not possible.

3. **ga**

When an interrogative word is the subject, it is marked by **ga**.

    Donata ga ikimasu ka.   *Who will go?*

    Nani ga arimasu ka.   *What is there (in that place)?*

    Itsu ga ii desu ka.   *When would it be convenient to you?*

    Doko ga shizuka desu ka.   *Which place is quiet?*

4. **ga**

In the subordinate clause of a complex sentence, **ga** is used as the subject marker.

Tanom-san <u>wa</u> kaerimashita.   *Mr. Tanom returned.*

Anata wa Tanom-san <u>ga</u> kaetta koto o shitte imasu ka.

Do you know that Mr. Tanom returned?

5. **wa**

wa sometimes indicates the sentence topic and may be used instead of **de, e, o, ni** or other particles.

1) **Anata no kaisha <u>wa</u> nani o tsukutte imasu ka.**
   (de)

   What do you produce in your company?

2) **Ginkō <u>wa</u> dō ittara ii desu ka.**
   (e)

   Which way should I take to go to the bank?

3) **Yasai <u>wa</u> tabemasu ga, niku <u>wa</u> tabemasen.**
   (o)   (o)

   I eat vegetables but I don't eat meat.

In this case, **wa** is used to mark two items being contrasted.

4) **Ano heya <u>wa</u> tomodachi ga sunde imasu.**
   (ni)

   My friend lives in that room.

Particle **de, e, ni**, except **o**, are often used together with **wa**, such as **dewa, ewa** or **niwa**.

Anata no kaisha <u>wa</u> nani o tsukutte imasu ka=

Anata no kaisha <u>dewa</u> nani o tsukutte imasu ka.

6. **wa**

wa is used when one distinguishes one case from another and clarifies the difference between them.

[watashi wa] Eigo <u>wa</u> wakarimasu ga, Supein-go <u>wa</u> wakarimasen.

I understand English, but don't understand Spanish.

[Ano hito wa] uta <u>wa</u> jōzu desu ga, dansu <u>wa</u> heta desu.

He is good at singing, but not good at dancing.

[watashi wa] sakana wa tabemasu ga, niku wa tabemasen.

I eat fish, but don't eat meat.

Dai 29 ka

All patterns involving verb structures which are treated in this book are listed in this lesson.

Dai 30 ka

Transformation of part of speech

1. **i**-adjective ⟶ adverb

   i-adjective may be changed into an adverb by replacing the last **i** with **ku.**

   > **hayai desu** *is quick*......**hayaku arukimasu** *walk quickly.*

2. **na**-adjective ⟶ adverb

   na-adjective may be changed into an adverb by attaching the particle **ni** to the stem.

   > **shizuka desu** *is quiet*.......**shizuka ni hanashimasu** *speak quietly.*

3. verb ⟶ noun

   Some verbs may be changed into nouns by removing the ending **masu.** Notice that this operation may not be applied to all verbs. V-(plain form) **koto,** for example **yasumu koto,** or **hanasu koto** are noun phrases which refer to action and differ in meaning from nouns formed by removal of **masu.**

   > **yasumimasu** *rest,*   **yasumi** *holiday,*   **yasumu koto** *resting,*
   > **hanashimasu** *speak,* **hanashi** *speech, story,* **hanasu koto** *speaking.*

4. **i**-adjective ⟶ noun

   i-adjective may be changed into a noun by replacing the last **i** with **sa.**

   > **omoi** *heavy*......**omosa** *weight*

5. ⟶ V-[masu] kata ⟵   *how to...*

   When **kata** is attached to the stem of a verb (i.e., the **masu**-form minus the **masu**), the verb is changed into a noun and means *the way to..., a method of...-ing.*

   > **yomimasu** *read*......**yomikata** *how to read.*

6.

$$\left.\begin{array}{l} \text{A-ku} \\ \text{Na} \\ \text{N} \end{array}\right\} \text{ni} \left.\vphantom{\begin{array}{l} \text{A-ku} \\ \text{Na} \\ \text{N} \end{array}}\right\} \boxed{\text{narimasu}} \qquad become\ldots$$

This pattern expresses a change of a state which happens naturally, or by itself. (Lesson 15)

ōkii desu *is big*......ōkiku narimasu *become big.*

shizuka desu *is quiet*......shizuka ni narimasu *become quiet.*

12-ji desu *It is 12 o'clock*......12-ji ni narimasu *It gets to be 12 o'clock.*

7.

$$\left.\begin{array}{l} \text{A-ku} \\ \text{Na} \\ \text{N} \end{array}\right\} \text{ni} \left.\vphantom{\begin{array}{l} \text{A-ku} \\ \text{Na} \\ \text{N} \end{array}}\right\} \boxed{\text{shimasu}} \qquad make\ (it)\ldots$$

This pattern expresses a change of a state which is brought about by somebody.

hayai desu *is fast*......hayaku shimasu *make it fast.*

shizuka desu *is quiet*......shizuka ni shimasu *get quiet down, make it quiet.*

ashita desu *It is tomorrow*......ashita ni shimasu *(we'll) make it tomorrow.*

(i.e. *we'll decide to do it tomorrow.*)

Index to Grammatical Notes

日 本 語 の 基 礎 I

＜文法解説書英語版＞　定価 1,550 円
（本体 1,505 円）

1975年9月5日　初版発行
1989年4月1日　第 10 刷

編　集　　財団法人 海 外 技 術 者 研 修 協 会

発　行　　株式会社 スリーエー ネットワーク
東京都千代田区猿楽町2丁目6番3号
電話 (03) 292-6191(代表)松栄ビル
郵便番号 101

印　刷　　奥 村 印 刷 株 式 会 社

不許複製　ISBN4-906224-13-X　C0081